THE RELIGIOUS THOUGHT
OF SAMUEL JOHNSON

Samuel Johnson

PORTRAIT BY JOHN OPIE

The Religious Thought
of
Samuel Johnson

Chester F. Chapin

Ann Arbor
The University of Michigan Press

to
William B. Dickens

Preface

In 1964 Professor Maurice J. Quinlan published his *Samuel Johnson: A Layman's Religion* (Madison, Wis.), the first book-length study of Johnson's religion to appear in our century.

Why, then, another book on the same subject? My principal justification is that I discuss matters not discussed by Quinlan, but matters, I think, of considerable interest to students of Johnson's moral and religious thought. Very properly in a book which is in some ways a pioneer study, Quinlan is concerned to define Johnson's attitude toward the principal doctrines and teachings of Christianity. Because Quinlan has demonstrated Johnson's essential orthodoxy on these matters, I take the orthodoxy for granted and attempt in this book to show—or at least to give some reasons—why orthodoxy appealed to Johnson.

Part I is roughly chronological. I try to indicate what sort of religious training Johnson received in early childhood and what was involved in his adolescent "revolt" against religion. I then move on to his year at Oxford and attempt an evaluation of his return to or "rediscovery" of religion. My next chapter outlines the general characteristics of the mature Johnson's religious faith—and shows how this faith differed from another orthodoxy, that Evangelical Anglicanism which, together with early Methodism, sought to reform the Church of England from within.

In Part II I abandon chronology in order to focus upon

specific aspects of Johnson's mature religious thought: in particular, his use of the Christian "evidences," the relationship in his thought between ethics and eschatology, his attitude toward the problems of evil, free will, and "necessity," his view of the proper relationship between church and state, and, finally, his attitude toward the non-Christian world.

I can give no very satisfactory explanation for my choice of topics. Others might have been chosen. I have tried, however, to include topics which were important to Johnson and his age—important because they posed problems for eighteenth-century orthodoxy. Some of these problems are perennial; others may be of limited relevance today. All orthodox Christian thinkers in every age must come to terms with the matters discussed in Chapters VI and VII; this is perhaps less true of the matters treated in Chapters V and VIII.

In general I have discussed these problems as Johnson and his age discussed them; that is, I have ignored modern discussion of the problem unless such discussion seemed helpful in clarifying for modern readers what Johnson and his contemporaries thought. In accordance with this approach, I have let Johnson, his contemporaries, and the authors of the books he read, speak for themselves. I have quoted much from Boswell, and Johnson, we know, often talked for victory—but only rarely, I think, when he was discussing religion.[1] Hence I have usually treated Johnson's remarks on religion in the *Life* as of equal authority with his written comments.

I have not discussed the question of Johnson's final religious position—the matter of his "late conversion"—because I believe with Robert Voitle that little of interest can now be advanced on this subject unless new evidence is forthcoming.[2]

My greatest debt is to books by Professors James L. Clifford and Donald J. Greene. I have differed with Clifford and Greene on occasion, but the earlier chapters of this book could hardly have been written without constant recourse to Clifford's *Young Sam Johnson* and Greene's *The Politics of Samuel Johnson*.

My thanks are due the Clarendon Press, Oxford, for permission to quote from the Hill-Powell edition of Boswell's

Preface

Life of Johnson (6 vols., 1934-50) and the R. W. Chapman edition of Johnson's *Letters* (3 vols., 1952); and to the Yale University Press for permission to quote from Johnson's *The Idler and The Adventurer*, edited by W. J. Bate, J. M. Bullitt, and L. F. Powell (New Haven, 1963).

I wish to thank Kay Voorhees, Betty Phillips, and Dorothy Strand for help in typing the manuscript.

Contents

Abbreviations and Short Titles

Clifford	James L. Clifford, *Young Sam Johnson* (New York, 1955).
DNB	*Dictionary of National Biography*
Greene	Donald J. Greene, *The Politics of Samuel Johnson* (New Haven, 1960).
JM	*Johnsonian Miscellanies*, ed. G. B. Hill, 2 vols. (Oxford, 1897).
Letter	Indicates reference by letter number (not by page) to *The Letters of Samuel Johnson*, ed. R. W. Chapman, 3 vols. (Oxford, 1952).
Life	Boswell's *Life of Johnson*, ed. Hill-Powell, 6 vols. (Oxford, 1934-50). Cited in the text by volume and page only; and in the footnotes as *Life*.
PMLA	*Publications of the Modern Language Association of America*.
Poems	*The Poems of Samuel Johnson*, ed. D. N. Smith and E. L. McAdam (Oxford, 1941).
Poets	Johnson's *Lives of the Poets*, ed. G. B. Hill, 3 vols. (New York, 1967).
Works, I	Johnson's *Diaries, Prayers, and Annals*, ed. E. L. McAdam with D. and M. Hyde (New Haven, 1958).
Works, II	Johnson's *The Idler and The Adventurer*, ed. W. J. Bate, *et al.* (New Haven, 1963).
Works (1825)	*The Works of Samuel Johnson*, 9 vols. (Oxford, 1825).

Books from Johnson's library are cited by item number as listed in A. Edward Newton's *Sale Catalogue of Dr. Johnson's Library* (New York, 1925).

Part I

Johnson's Earliest Instruction in Religion

KNOWING SOMETHING OF THE RELIGIOUS ATTITUDES of Samuel Johnson's parents, scholars have naturally attempted an assessment of the influence these may have had in shaping Johnson's mature religious outlook. Maurice Quinlan, impressed as he is with the influence of William Law's *Serious Call to a Devout and Holy Life*, which Johnson first encountered at Oxford, omits all discussion of specifically parental influence in his *Samuel Johnson: A Layman's Religion*. But the matter does receive brief treatment in two standard works on Johnson, James Clifford's *Young Sam Johnson* and Donald Greene's *The Politics of Samuel Johnson*.

So far as Johnson's father Michael is concerned, the only question at issue is Michael's supposed Jacobitism. It is admitted on all sides today that Michael's son was no Jacobite, that his sympathy for certain aspects of James the Second's religion by no means turned him into a crypto-Roman Catholic, that the mature Johnson was, in short, a solid Church of England man. But within that comprehensive national church there were many shades of opinion. If Michael was a Jacobite, as both Boswell and Sir John Hawkins maintain,[1] was this a factor in the development of Samuel's political and religious conservatism? Boswell implies that it was. But all surviving testimony on this matter is of questionable value. Neither

Hawkins nor Boswell had firsthand knowledge of Johnson's early years and, as Donald Greene points out, there is a "countertradition" which insists that Michael Johnson was a good Whig.[2]

How much did Johnson himself know of his father's political and religious opinions? This is surely the crucial question in any assessment of paternal influence. We may note, first of all, that Johnson never called his father a Jacobite. The term itself is not included in his *Dictionary*. Johnson had perhaps a lexicographical preference for the more exact term "nonjuror," which he defines as "one who, conceiving James II unjustly deposed, refuses to swear allegiance to those who have succeeded him." Now Michael, whatever his private opinions, had taken the oaths of allegiance to Queen Anne and George I, and so far as we know never engaged in any activity, overt or covert, in behalf of the Jacobite cause. The only explicit statement we have from Johnson himself is the remark he made, after Boswell had "pressed" him, that the decision to take the oaths was a matter Michael "was to settle with himself" (II, 322). This may indicate that Johnson suspected his father of Jacobite sympathies; what it indicates as well, I think, is that Johnson did not know for certain just *what* his father's sentiments were. Michael Johnson was not a communicative man. Often away from home and often silent when at home, it seems unlikely that he would have unburdened himself of Jacobite sentiments even in the bosom of his family. The word might get about, with undesirable consequences. This would seem the more likely if, as Boswell thought, Michael took the oaths for purely prudential "business" reasons. But this is perhaps a libelous inference. There is no evidence that the "pious and worthy" Michael, as Johnson called him,[3] was less than honorable, and it would require no very delicate sense of honor for Michael to believe that having taken the oaths he had a moral obligation to keep to himself whatever Jacobite sentiments he may have held.

In all the external facts of his career of which we have knowledge Michael Johnson emerges as a solid Church of England man, thoroughly devoted to the Protestant succession.

4

One of Johnson's earliest memories was that of being taken to London by his mother, Sarah, to be "touched" by Queen Anne for the cure of his scrofula (the so-called "King's Evil"). This ceremony had been allowed to lapse under King William, and its immediate revival under Anne was, as James Clifford has said, "a means of asserting her hereditary right to the throne, in contrast to the parliamentary authority of William and the Hanoverians."[4] But Anne's revival of the "royal touch" was also a defiance of Jacobite claims. It said in effect that Anne was as legitimate a sovereign as James II. Denying this, the Jacobites denied that the power of the royal touch descended to Mary, William, or Anne. It resided only in James and in the line of succession established by his son, the Pretender, and so we find "Henry IX," the "last of the Stuarts," touching for the "King's Evil" throughout his "reign" (1788-1807), long after most Englishmen, including the most ardent of high churchmen, had relegated the practice to the dustbin of outworn superstitions.[5] Now there is no evidence that Michael was less convinced than his wife Sarah of the efficacy of the royal touch as administered by Anne as against the claim that the power resided only in James and the Jacobite succession. Sarah's trip to London entailed considerable trouble and expense which Michael apparently bore without complaint, although he could discourage Sarah from social entertainments because of the high price of tea.[6]

It was the custom when a person was "touched" for Queen Anne to place a golden amulet about his neck. Johnson wore his "touchpiece" for many years, perhaps for the rest of his life. This may indicate, as A. L. Reade has said, that Johnson "always retained a good measure of superstition" as to the efficacy of the royal touch.[7] One may be entitled, as well, to see a kind of religious symbolism in the practice, a symbolic indication of Johnson's—and his parents'—solid attachment to the Church of England as against the threat from the right (the Jacobites) and from the left (those Whigs and their allies, whether dissenters or low churchmen, who agitated for a curtailment of church authority or privilege). Whatever Boswell may have thought, Johnson seems never to have regarded such a position as sectarian, to be singled out for classification as "high Tory," or even "high" church as opposed to "low." He seems to have regarded it, rather, as a middle-of-the-road position, excluding the extremes of sectarian or party zeal whether of the right or of the left.

But the most important reason for doubting whether Michael's conversation or example had any significant effect on the development of Johnson's religious outlook is the fact that, as Clifford says, young Sam's "earliest instruction, religious and secular, came from his mother,"[8] not from Michael. And here, interestingly enough, instead of influence supposedly working toward the development of a conservative, high church position, what evidence there is indicates, as Greene says, that the Fords, Sarah's family, had "distinct leanings toward what would now be called the Low Church and its political counterpart, Whiggism."[9] But granted such leanings, I cannot find they had any effect upon the religious instruction young Sam received from his mother or, to put it another way, I see no reason to suppose this earliest instruction —and I emphasize the word "earliest"—would have varied in any significant particular had Sarah's relations been solidly high church and Tory. What Johnson received was instruction in what might be called "basic Anglicanism," a kind of instruction which pious Anglicans, both high and low church, would have endorsed.

But let us turn to Johnson's own account of the earliest religious instruction he could remember having received from Sarah. This was shortly after the trip to be "touched," when he was three years old:

> I suppose that in this year [1712] I was first informed of a future state. I remember, that being in bed with my mother one morning, I was told by her of the two places to which the inhabitants of this world were received after death; one a fine place filled with happiness, called Heaven; the other a *sad* place, called Hell. That this account much affected my imagination, I do not remember. When I was risen, my mother bade me repeat what she had told me to Thomas Jackson [the family servant].

When I told this afterwards to my mother, she seemed to wonder that she should begin such talk so late as that the first time could be remembered. (*Works*, I, 10)

Professor Clifford remarks of this incident (*Young Sam Johnson*, p. 23):

If he was too young at this time to grasp the full significance of what his mother was saying, she must subsequently have made the dangers of future punishment clear enough. Sarah's approach to the Bible was literal and devout. Since her own father's taste in reading had run to evangelical sermons, it may be that she had absorbed some of his Calvinism. Hell was real, and damnation no mere symbolic device. So well did her son learn the lesson that he was never rid of the terrors of the other world.

Although in this passage Clifford is not using the terms "evangelical" and "Calvinism" in any strict doctrinal sense, it may be well to point out the Church of England's relationship to certain doctrines often thought characteristic of Calvinist teaching. If an emphasis on the doctrines of original sin and justification by faith alone be considered characteristic of such teaching, then the Church of England, according to her articles of faith, is solidly "Calvinist" (see Articles 11 through 15 of the Thirty-nine Articles). But an emphasis upon the doctrine of predestination has been most commonly considered the distinguishing mark of the Calvinist; here the framers of the Book of Common Prayer, in their attempts to "comprehend" predestinarians within the fold of the national church, wrote a long and somewhat equivocal article (Art. 17), the upshot of which is that Anglicans may or may not believe in the doctrines of "Predestination and Election."

But if Sarah's "Calvinism" refers merely to the fact that her approach to the Bible was "literal and devout," that she believed in a very real hell and taught this belief to Sam, then she believed and taught only what thousands of orthodox middle-class women believed and taught to their children, then and for many generations thereafter, whether "Calvinist," "evangelical," or strictly "high church." A book which Sarah

7

used in instructing young Sam in the duties of religion was the enormously popular anonymous work, *The Whole Duty of Man* (first published in 1657), commonly ascribed to the royalist divine, Richard Allestree.[10] We must consider this work in some detail later; for the moment we may note that its author, early recognized as "a true and sincere friend of the Church of England,"[11] was heartily damned by men like William Cowper because he seemed to slight doctrines dear to the evangelical heart.[12] But the description of hell in the *Whole Duty* is as "literal" as anything to be found in evangelical or Calvinist literature, and fully bears out A. L. Reade's account of the conventional hell of the period as "a vast incinerator with an unlimited supply of fuel and toasting forks."[13] In view of the fact that Sarah evidently *began* her religious instruction with talk of heaven and hell, it is interesting to note that Allestree follows precisely the same procedure. This was probably standard practice based upon the common sense prescription that if one is to teach someone, even a child, that religion requires him to act in a certain way and not otherwise, then the sanctions that underlie such requirements ought to be clearly impressed upon his memory, or as Allestree puts it (preface, sect. 1), " 'tis in vain to tell men their Duty, till they be perswaded of the necessity of performing it." And these persuasives to duty, in Allestree's account, are formidable enough! In his preface, "Shewing the Necessity of Caring for the Soul," he remarks that

> if you have any true kindness to your Body, shew it by taking Care of your Souls. Think with your selves, how you will be able to endure Everlasting Burnings. If a small spark of fire, lighting on the least part of the body, be so intolerable, what will it be to have the Whole cast into the hottest flames? And that not so for some few hours or days, but for ever? So that when you have spent many Thousands of years in that unspeakable Torment, you shall be no nearer coming out of it, than you were the First day you went in. (sect. 6)

It is misleading to regard Sarah's unimaginative and literal approach to religion as the product of "evangelical" or Calvinist influence. What we have here is simple Protestant fundamentalism, a fundamentalism shared by the vast majority of the orthodox middle classes, whether Baptist, Presbyterian, or Anglican. At the same time it may be admitted that if Sarah had absorbed something of the Calvinist approach to religion, she may have taken a "harder line" with Sam on the subject of future punishment than would have been usual. But her conception of hell, in any case, would have been literal enough.

When we turn to Sarah's relatives, we encounter the case of Mrs. Harriots, Sarah's rich cousin, whom Michael once offended "by sending his horses from home on Sunday," which she considered a "breach of duty." Johnson agreed that it *was* a breach of duty, and in his diary many years later he singled out Mrs. Harriots' family as remarkable for the "regularity" of its religious observances. According to Donald Greene, "the point seems to be that Mrs. Harriots, with Puritanical and hence Sabbatarian leanings, regarded Sunday travel as an infraction of religious obligation, a prejudice which Michael, as a 'High Churchman,' delighted to flout."[14] It may be so, but a disapproval of Sunday travel was hardly a Puritan "prejudice" exclusively. It was a law of Charles II that "all hackney coaches were forbidden to ply their trade on Sunday," and, according to Lecky, "the travelling of waggons and stage coaches on that day was during the first half of the eighteenth century almost, if not altogether, unknown in England."[15] And it was during the reign of Queen Anne that the Society for the Reformation of Manners, composed of both Anglicans and dissenters, instituted "tens of thousands of successful prosecutions," a number of which were "for swearing and for travelling on Sunday."[16]

How strict a Sabbatarian was Sarah herself? Johnson's remark about the "regularity" of Mrs. Harriots' family hardly indicates that he thought his own parents remarkably strict in their religious observances. Johnson tells us that from about his ninth to his fourteenth year he did not go to church at all, but used to go and read in the fields on Sundays. The church at Lichfield was under repair, and Sam was supposed to find a seat in other churches, but having bad eyes and "being aukward about this" he apparently persuaded his parents to allow him to forego church-going altogether.[17] Strict Sabbatarians would surely consider the omission of church attendance a more serious "breach of duty" than traveling on Sunday.

The mature Johnson was a great admirer of the Anglican Book of Common Prayer, and had apparently committed great parts of it to memory.[18] The process which led to this began early. "When he was a child in petticoats, and had learnt to read," Boswell tells us,

> Mrs. Johnson one morning put the common prayer-book into his hands, pointed to the collect for the day, and said, 'Sam, you must get this by heart.' She went up stairs, leaving him to study it: But by the time she had reached the second floor, she heard him following her. 'What's the matter?' said she. 'I can say it,' he replied; and repeated it distinctly, though he could not have read it over more than twice. (I, 40)

The collects were not the only part of the Prayer Book that young Sam was made to get by heart. Before he entered Lichfield Grammar School at the age of almost seven and a half, he had mastered his Catechism, the most important parts of which are the Apostles' Creed, the Lord's Prayer, and the Ten Commandments. Here Sarah was mindful of the injunction laid down by the author of *The Whole Duty of Man*, that

> it nearly concerns every Parent, as they will free themselves from the guilt of their Childrens undoing, that they be careful to see them instructed in all necessary things; to which purpose it will be fit early to teach them some short Catechism, of which none so fit as the Church Catechism (chap. 2, sect. 26).

"None so fit" because, as a popular commentary on the Prayer Book explained, the Church Catechism is "so short that the youngest children may learn it by heart; and yet so full, that it contains all things necessary to be known in order to salvation."[19] The Lord's Prayer, the Apostles' Creed, and the Ten Commandments—these are the basic texts of Anglican faith, and in orthodox households were apparently drilled into children at a very early age. Laetitia Hawkins, the daughter of Johnson's friend Sir John, believed that every child of three years old "may learn" the Lord's Prayer, and was horrified, many years after Johnson's death, to hear of a certain criminal who was found to be "ignorant not only of the Ten Commandments and the Creed, but of that which it is hardly possible not to know, the Lord's prayer."[20] And Johnson himself was much surprised to find when he first entered school that one of his classmates had never been taught his Catechism. (*Works*, I, 13)

But compulsory drill in the first elements of religion, however beneficial in training the memory, is not likely to have much effect upon a small boy's conduct unless the parent can adapt such instruction to the understanding of the child, and can show its relevance to the particular situation in which the child finds himself. It is in this department that Sarah most notably failed. As Clifford says, "she was always trying to teach him rigid ideas of morality and behavior, but her admonitions rarely went beyond empty formulas." "My mother," Johnson told Mrs. Thrale, "was always telling me that I did not *behave* myself properly; that I should endeavour to learn *behaviour*, and such cant: but when I replied, that she ought to tell me what to do, and what to avoid, her admonitions were commonly, for that time at least, at an end."[21]

Perhaps it was because she felt herself deficient in this regard that Sarah decided to supplement her own admonitions by those of a recognized authority in the field. Or perhaps she was simply following popular precedent. Johnson told Boswell

that Sunday was a heavy day to him when he was young. His mother made him read the Whole Duty of Man on that day; & when he read for instance the Chapter on theft he was no more convinced that theft was wrong than before; so there was no accession of ideas—He said that a boy should be introduced to such Books by being directed to the Arrangement, to the style, to other excellencies; & he would of course attend to the doctrine

—that the mind would not weary, if directed thus to various subjects.[22]

The title page of the *Whole Duty* reads as follows: "The Whole Duty of Man, laid down in a plain and familiar way for the Use of All, but especially the Meanest Reader. Divided into Seventeen Chapters: One whereof being read every Lords Day, the Whole may be read over Thrice in the Year. Necessary for all Families." The chapters themselves are entitled "Sundays" to emphasize the author's recommendation for the proper use of the book. Sarah, we may believe, was not very imaginative or original in her educational methods; had she followed the author's directions for one year only, Sam, given his remarkable memory, would have been quite familiar with the book even though he resented his task and derived little instruction from it.

The *Whole Duty* is essentially a religious "conduct" book. As the preface has it (sect. 1): "The only intent of this ensuing Treatise, is to be a short and Plain Direction to the very meanest Readers, to behave themselves so in this world, that they may be happy for ever in the next." Allestree assumes his readers have a sufficient knowledge of the major doctrines of Christianity, doctrines we have seen Sarah impressing upon Sam when he was little more than a baby. Since the book deals with Christian ethics and avoids matters of theological controversy, it could be acceptable to families other than Anglican. The young David Hume, who came of a Scottish Presbyterian family, once went to the extent of abstracting a list of vices from the book in order to test his character against them, "leaving out Murder and Theft and such vices as he had no chance of committing, having no inclination to commit them."[23] But perhaps the most striking indication of the popularity of the book is the existence of a petition addressed to Queen Anne's Lord Lieutenant in Ireland, in which it is seriously proposed that the book be translated into Irish as a means of promoting "the conversion of the Popish natives to the Protestant religion."[24]

It was popular because it fulfilled a need. The vast corpus

of seventeenth-century divinity was often controversial or polemical in nature, or was addressed to a learned audience, and hence full of allusions not only to scripture but to the church fathers and to classical and Renaissance writers not likely to be known by the "meanest Reader." The *Whole Duty* had the practical merit of setting forth in relatively short compass and in plain English and non-polemical fashion a rather complete system of Christian ethics based firmly upon the Bible and the Book of Common Prayer.

Although he thought his mother made an unwise use of it so far as he was concerned, Johnson in later life thought enough of the *Whole Duty* to recommend it in a list of what we might call "basic books" which he wrote out for the use of a young man "as to his studies" (IV, 311).[25] Nevertheless, I would not want to argue that a book which he was forced to read as a distasteful task had any considerable influence upon him. But I would maintain that he was thoroughly familiar with its contents.

There has been a tendency, which began in Johnson's own day, to look beyond the popular Anglicanism of his youth for the origins of certain of his characteristic religious emphases. Sir John Hawkins gives perhaps the best statement of this point of view. Johnson's religion, he says,

> had a tincture of enthusiasm, arising, as it is conjectured, from the fervour of his imagination, and the perusal of St. Augustine and other of the fathers, and the writings of Kempis and the ascetics, which prompted him to the employment of composing meditations and devotional exercises. It further produced in him an habitual reverence for the name of God, which he was never known to utter but on proper occasions and with due respect . . . and, lastly, it inspired him with that charity, meaning thereby a general concern for the welfare of all mankind, without which we are told that all pretensions to religion are vain. (*Life of Johnson*, pp. 162-63)

There is, I think, much truth in this statement. Johnson's religion was never a static affair, something he learned at his mother's knee and never thereafter "revised," as it were. But we are concerned here only with what Johnson *did* learn at his mother's knee, and it is possible that Sir John's statement might be interpreted (I think contrary to his intention) to mean that Johnson *first* encountered an emphasis upon the necessity of reverence for the name of God or of Christian charity in the writings of the fathers, the ascetics, or, we may add, in those of William Law, whose *Serious Call to a Devout and Holy Life*, a work thoroughly within the ascetic tradition, first inspired Johnson to think seriously of religion. It is not that such writings—and others—may not have had a much more profound effect upon Johnson than the *Whole Duty;* the point is that he would find in them no important Christian duty or obligation that Allestree (himself a learned man, thoroughly acquainted with the fathers) had not also inculcated, however sketchily.

I confine myself to certain of Johnson's religious attitudes which impressed his contemporaries as in some way unusual or especially characteristic of the man. Everyone is aware of Johnson's religious horror of unnecessary oaths, and, as Hawkins puts it, of his "habitual reverence for the name of God." Allestree's fourth chapter is entirely devoted to this matter. I quote his "argument" in full: "Honour due to Gods name; Sins against it; Blasphemy, Swearing, Assertory Oaths, Promissory Oaths, unlawful Oaths, and the Sin of them." We know of Johnson's concern over his failure to rise early. Although no ascetic, Allestree, like William Law after him, stresses the importance of "Temperance in Sleep" and warns against the "Mischiefs of Sloth" (chap. 9). We know of the serious self-examination which preceded Johnson's reception of the Eucharist. Allestree might have been speaking directly to men of Johnson's "scruples" in this regard. In his third chapter (sect. 21), although stressing the importance of serious self-examination, Allestree directs himself primarily to those he considers over-scrupulous, too fearful of their own unworthiness. Such men, he says, should lay their case before a minister of religion and abide by his decision. Finally, and most important of all, there is the matter of Johnson's Christian charity, which some of his friends thought went beyond the call of duty. Here, if we may speak metaphorically, the emphasis given to this duty in Allestree matches that given it in Johnson's own life. Allestree divided his book into three parts. The first concerns our duty to God (chaps. 1-5), the second, our duty to ourselves (chaps. 6-9), and the third, our duty to our neighbors (chaps. 10-17). While the final, climactic chapter is wholly devoted to the great duty of Christian charity, so, in a sense, is the whole final section, over one-third of the book, as Allestree himself recognizes when stressing "that grand rule of *Loving our Neighbours as our selves.*" This, he says, "the Apostle makes the sum of our whole duty to our Neighbours" (chap. 17, sect. 14).

The only thing unusual about many, perhaps most, of Johnson's religious attitudes is the seriousness with which he entertained them. They are endorsed by the popular Anglicanism of Johnson's childhood as well as by the classics of Christian literature outside the Anglican tradition, with which he later became familiar.

Summing up the nature of the religious instruction Johnson received from his mother, I would emphasize that I am not considering his reaction to that instruction or what he may have learned outside the home or through his voluntary reading, but only that to which he was exposed under compulsion. I conclude that it is misleading to use words such as "low church," "high church," "Puritan," "evangelical," or "Calvinist" in connection with this parental instruction. As I have said, the only proper term would appear to be something like "basic Anglicanism," and for a definition of this we may follow a recent student of Anglican devotion who concludes that in the first half of the eighteenth century, "Anglicanism meant in doctrine the Bible and the Prayer Book, in practice *The Whole Duty of Man.*"[26]

Childhood and Adolescence

It is generally recognized today that some form of adolescent rebellion against parental authority is a normal stage in the process of growing up. Even in families where there is a minimum of child-parent conflict, maturation would seem to imply some degree of resistance to parental dicta. Parental ideas must be earned; that is, they must be tested against the developing mind and experience of the child as he moves out of the family circle into the world at large. They may survive this test well enough. The child, let us say, may accept the religion of his parents, but mature acceptance—as against the unquestioning acceptance of early childhood—must mean that the child has found the religious values of his parents meaningful with regard to his *own* experience of life. As a modern psychologist puts it, "the youth is compelled to transform his religious attitudes—indeed all his attitudes—from second-hand fittings to first-hand fittings of his personality. He can no longer let his parents do his thinking for him. Although in some cases the transition is fluent and imperceptible, more often there is a period of rebellion."[1]

In Johnson's case there *was* such a period of rebellion, in the opinion of some critics so intense as to have had lasting, even traumatic effects. According to George Irwin, Sarah, a woman impossible to please, nagged young Sam constantly, withheld the praise his affectionate nature required, and drummed into him a sense of his own worthlessness. As a consequence, the mature Johnson suffered from "subliminal mother-hate." Never able to convince himself that he loved his mother as he ought, he suffered from powerful guilt feelings whenever he thought of her, feelings which formed no small addition to the variety of other ills, mental and physical, which dogged him through life.[2] Irwin may be right, although I believe his conclusion requires him to posit a degree of tyranny on Sarah's part unwarranted by the evidence.

But without going as far as Irwin, we may note a few obvious facts. The childless Sarah was forty when Sam was born. At her age and with her lack of experience in caring for small children she would have had her problems with Sam, even had she been endowed with qualities of mind and temperament more suitable for such a task. Moreover, Sarah was faced with a problem few mothers have to cope with. She had given birth to a child prodigy. Some precocious children are tractable enough, but Sam was not one of them. The combative spirit manifests itself very early in the surviving anecdotes of his childhood, and was aggravated by his consciousness of his physical disabilities. He could not excel other boys on the play-field, but he soon discovered in the world of books a means of asserting his superiority. From the time he entered school it could be said of him, as he said himself of his year at Oxford, that he sought to fight his way by his "literature" (I, 74). Hating to apply himself more than he had to, he was nevertheless very proud of his scholarship and envious of boys he saw as possible rivals to his intellectual supremacy.

Precocious, combative, insatiably curious but easily bored, he was undoubtedly, in the cant phrase, a "difficult" child. The result is predictable enough. As he emerged from early childhood, the period of unquestioning acceptance, toward adolescence, the period of self-assertion and independent thought, he found his mother's religious regimen more and more stultifying. Dull tasks, unimaginatively enforced, acted to repress rather than to enliven his interest in religion, and for some years he tended to shy away from it as a subject associated in his mind with all that was irksome and boring. One may assume, also, an early awareness of his mother's intellectual limitations. Children, especially precocious children, sense these things. He later said that he did not respect his mother, and the literal-minded Sarah, "unacquainted with books," was only too vulnerable a target for his youthful wit. The wit and the lack of respect are equally evident in the famous reply when, having been called a puppy, he asked Sarah if she knew what they called a puppy's mother. His maturing ego and sense of intellectual superiority found gratification—and revenge for "heavy" Sundays—in the discovery that "it was fun to shock his mother with skeptical remarks."[3]

"Skeptical remarks," yes, but Johnson's revolt was not against religion as such, or was so in a sense requiring careful qualification. Johnson himself refers to this period on two separate occasions. He told Boswell that from about his ninth to his fourteenth year, when the church at Lichfield was under repair and he used to read in the fields on Sundays, he was "unattentive to or indifferent about religion." Somewhat later, perhaps after his fourteenth year when he was again required to attend church, he passed over to a more negative stance. He became "a sort of lax talker" against religion although he did not much think against it, and this lasted till he went to Oxford "where it would not be suffered."[4] Again, speaking of roughly the same period, Johnson remarked (IV, 215, n. 5) that from his tenth until his twenty-second year he was "totally regardless of religion." It had "dropped out" of his mind. These statements are not, I think, contradictory. Given the mature Johnson's high conception of what it meant to be truly religious, indifference or lax talk against religion, even if one did not *think* against it, were manifestations of a condition in which the individual was, for all practical purposes, "totally regardless" of religion.

But we should not take these statements quite at face value. Indeed, there is some indication that Johnson's youthful indifference was in part a result of his religious concern. During his tenth year when, he tells us, religion had dropped out of his mind, a curious incident occurred which Johnson, fully aware of its strangeness, confided only to his wife, to his lifelong friend John Taylor, and to Mrs. Thrale. According to Mrs. Thrale's account,

> at the age of ten years his mind was disturbed by scruples of infidelity, which preyed upon his spirits, and made him very uneasy; the more so, as he revealed his uneasiness to no one, being naturally (as he said) 'of a sullen temper and reserved disposition.' He searched, however, diligently but fruitlessly, for evidences of the truth of revelation; and at length recollecting a book he had once seen in his father's shop, intitled, *De Veritate Religionis* [by Hugo Grotius], he began to think himself highly culpable for neglecting such a means of information . . . . but on examination, not finding himself scholar enough to peruse its contents, set his heart at rest; and, not thinking to enquire whether there were any English books written on the subject, followed his usual amusements, and considered his conscience as lightened of a crime.
> (*JM*, I, 157-58)

As Professor Clifford says, "at least he knew that someone more learned than himself had wrestled with similar doubts and conquered them." In view of the mature Johnson's fear of death, it is interesting to note that this boyish "scruple of infidelity" concerned doubts as to the "soul's immortality." And how did he resolve these doubts? "From the pain which guilt had given him, he now began to deduce the soul's immortality"; that is, he reasoned that if God had not intended eternal life for the human race, He would not afflict Sam Johnson with painful guilt feelings for presuming to doubt the truth of the doctrine. As Clifford says, "a boy of ten is not always logical or rational," and "this foolish Story," as Johnson called it, may well have reflected a mode of boyish reasoning by which "his skepticism was quieted for a few years."[5] Reassured, then, as to the fundamental truths of Christianity, the young Johnson could, in a sense, afford to neglect religion. He could afford to gratify his adolescent ego with clever remarks and skeptical objections when confronted with Sarah's platitudes, and since others wiser than himself were convinced of these fundamental truths he could, relying on their authority, excuse himself from thinking seriously of a subject that for him had been a source of irritation, boredom, and "uneasiness."

Such an attitude is hardly "skeptical" in any clearly definable philosophical or theological sense. It is a reaction directed more against Sarah and "authority" than against religion. If Johnson hated compulsory churchgoing and set tasks, he did not confuse these, even at this early age, with the essence of religion, and when he had doubts concerning the central doctrines of orthodox faith he was much disturbed and did what he could to allay them.

His boyish concern over the doctrine of immortality, which was "the point that belief first stopped at," reminds us of his statement many years later that "he never had a moment in which death was not terrible to him" (III, 153). And terrible it may have been to him, even at this early period, but only when he thought of it. If religion tended to remind him of the problem of death, this then was another reason for averting his attention from it. And there is reason to believe that the attempt was relatively successful. That his health was comparatively good until his twentieth year is confirmed by his own statement and that of his boyhood friend Edmund Hector.[6] He had not yet suffered from the severe fits of mental depression that later afflicted him, and he had not yet encountered the disappointments and struggles that followed hard upon his abortive career at Oxford. On the contrary, the years of adolescence, culminating in the happy opportunity of an Oxford education, were years of relatively hopeful and successful endeavor. Since Clifford has described these years in detail, when young Sam Johnson was becoming known in Lichfield as a youth of "parts" and was making the acquaintance of such men of wit and substance as Cornelius Ford and Gilbert Walmsley, we need only make the application—that Johnson, like many another ambitious adolescent, found it relatively easy to avert his thoughts from "futurity" when the present world presented such an interesting and hopeful appearance.

But religion was never far below the surface of his mind. Interesting as an indication of what Clifford calls Johnson's "submerged religious feeling"[7] at this time is the poem he wrote at the age of seventeen in celebration of the feast of St. Simon and St. Jude. Although this was almost certainly a school exercise and hence not an entirely voluntary effort, its "romantic ardor" breathes a spirit of youthful admiration for the constancy and devotion of these two Christian apostles

> To whom the church each rolling year
> Her solemn honours pays.

When Johnson remarked that he had been totally regardless of religion from his tenth until his twenty-second year, he added that sickness had brought it back to him, whereupon William Seward "wondered" that sickness and the view of death did not make more men religious. Johnson replied: "They do not know how to go about it: they have not the first notion. A man who has never had religion before, no more grows religious when he is sick, than a man who has never learnt figures can count when he has need of calculation" (IV, 216). In the sense of never having been exposed to it, it would have been hard to find a man among the literate classes in eighteenth-century England who had never "had religion." We are accustomed to think of this century as the age of Enlightenment, a time when orthodox religious beliefs were breaking down before the impact of a pervasive secularism, and certainly the age is as much that of Hume and Gibbon as of Johnson. Yet religion was much more a part of the fabric of everyday life than it is today, at least among the literate classes. In particular, nearly everyone in childhood received much the same sort of religious training. It is not surprising that both Hume and Gibbon were religious as boys; like children everywhere they accepted the values and beliefs of the society around them. Johnson spoke for the century as a whole when, commenting on the eschatology of *Paradise Lost*, he remarked that

> these truths are too important to be new: they have been
> taught to our infancy; they have mingled with our soli-

tary thoughts and familiar conversation, and are habitually interwoven with the whole texture of life.[8]

This being so, we are not surprised to find that religion is a factor in shaping the outlook even of those who rejected it. Thus Norman Kemp Smith can say of Hume:

> There is no question that at an early age Hume shed the whole body of Calvinist teaching [in which he had been raised.] It continued, however, to typify for him what he meant by religion; and owing to the very strength of the aversion which he had come to feel towards it, it was an important factor in determining the contrary character of the beliefs to which, as his philosophy matured, he definitively committed himself.[9]

The point of emphasizing the difference between the eighteenth century and our own more secular age is that the eighteenth-century intellectual, and by this term I mean anyone who was accustomed to think seriously of the world and of man's place in it, had at some point to come to terms with religion. There were those of course, then as now, to whom religion was a matter of little or no concern. But this was hardly true of the more powerful minds of the century, if only because religion still "overlapped," as it were, so many areas of intellectual interest. Considerable areas of science and philosophy had yet to free themselves from assumptions derived, in one way or another, from traditional interpretations of the Bible. The eighteenth-century intellectual, then, could not simply ignore religion. But the intellectual today may rather easily ignore it. Religion may form no part of his boyhood experience, and he may find in science or in a thoroughly secularized humanism an explanation of the world and of man's place in it which satisfies him so completely that the idea of looking elsewhere for "explanations" hardly occurs to him. But even if he is not attracted to science or to any particular brand of humanism, his contact with religion is often so slight that he normally turns elsewhere for the fulfillment of those needs, emotional or intellectual, which religion has traditionally claimed to satisfy. Professor Wallace Matson of Cornell reports the instance of a colleague of his who, "when asked to appear as a representative of atheism in a panel discussion, replied that he was not enough interested in religion even to be an atheist."[10]

This sort of indifference to religion was virtually impossible for the eighteenth-century intellectual, whatever his personal beliefs. There is none of it, certainly, in Hume and Gibbon, the great exemplars of the Enlightenment in eighteenth-century Britain. Their ultimate agnosticism or deism, as the case may be, followed hard upon an intense concern with religion as adolescents. To put it crudely, they had "tried religion" and found it wanting. The young Gibbon's progress from Anglicanism to Roman Catholicism to "philosophy" is well known from the account in his *Autobiography*. Hume, writing in 1751, describes his own struggles with religion:

> Any propensity you imagine I have to the other Side [i.e. in favour of the sceptical views of Philo in the *Dialogues concerning Natural Religion*] crept in upon me against my will: And tis not long ago that I burn'd an old Manuscript Book, wrote before I was twenty, which contained, Page after Page, the gradual Progress of my Thoughts on that head. It begun with an anxious Search after Arguments, to confirm the common Opinion: Doubts stole in, dissipated, return'd, were again dissipated, return'd again; and it was a perpetual Struggle of a restless Imagination against Inclination, perhaps against Reason.[11]

If I stress the point that the eighteenth-century intellectual had to take religion seriously, whatever his reaction to it, I do so to indicate, first, that Johnson's concern with religion is not an anomaly; second, that we could not expect Johnson to continue long inattentive or indifferent to religion. He had eventually to come to grips with it in a more serious way than he had yet done.

Meanwhile he was unknowingly preparing himself for his future eminence as a man of letters. Johnson was nineteen when he entered Oxford, but he is said to have told Bennet Langton that "his great period of study was from the age of twelve to that of eighteen," and he told Boswell that he "read very hard" as a young man and knew almost as much at eighteen as he did in the years of his maturity: "My judgment, to be sure," he added, "was not so good; but, I had all the facts." During his seventeenth and eighteenth years he read, "not voyages and travels, but all literature, Sir, all ancient writers, all manly; though but little Greek, only some of Anacreon and Hesiod; but in this irregular manner (added he) I had looked into a great many books, which were not commonly known at the Universities, where they seldom read any books but what are put into their hands by their tutors."[12] The "ancient writers" are primarily the Latin classics; Johnson at seventeen read Latin as easily as during the years of his maturity. The library that he brought with him to Oxford, culled largely from the shelves of his father's bookshop, confirms, and adds to, this report of his literary tastes. The Greek and Latin classics, together with such Latin poets of the Renaissance as George Buchanan and John Barclay, are heavily represented. Most of the English writers are poets, from Spenser down to Pope, with the Restoration and Queen Anne poets prominently featured: Milton, Dryden, Butler, Waller, Rowe, Garth, Prior, Addison, Philips, Blackmore, and Young. From the evidence of this collection it is clear that his taste ran chiefly to poetry, both Latin and English. If we compare this collection with the library auctioned off after his death, what is immediately striking is the absence of collections of sermons and other professedly religious works. Of a collection of well over one hundred volumes, only some eight or ten are specifically religious or devotional. There is a Bible, a Book of Common Prayer, two Greek testaments, and two popular devotional works: William Sherlock's *Practical Discourse concerning Death* and Robert Nelson's *The Great Duty of Frequenting the Christian Sacrifice*. There are also two poems on religious subjects: Edward

Young's *The Last Day* and Sir Richard Blackmore's *Creation:
A Philosophical Poem*.[13]

It may be appropriate to point out what Johnson would
find in these works, especially since, taken together, they
stress themes and reflect arguments typical of Anglican apologetics and devotional writing during the reign of Queen
Anne. All were well known to the reading public. Sherlock's
Discourse (1689), eulogized in a poem by Prior and praised
by Addison as "one of the strongest Persuasives to a Religious
Life that ever was written,"[14] had gone through nineteen editions by 1723; Nelson's *Great Duty* (1706) achieved a ninth
edition in 1727. Young's *Last Day* was immediately popular
in Tory and ministerial circles on its publication in 1713
(Young's fulsome dedication to the Queen—who is pictured
soaring away to regions of eternal bliss—also praises the peace
of Utrecht). Even Blackmore's *Creation*, also praised by
Addison (in *Spectator* 339), had a great, if short-lived success,
on its appearance early in 1712.[15]

Sherlock's *Discourse* is designed to prove that the only
preservative against the fear of death is a moral, Christian
life. Only the good man has nothing to fear at the Day of
Judgment, and here Sherlock sounds a note that we find
the mature Johnson sounding again and again—that a man
must be prepared for death at every moment of his life since
he can never know when he may be called by God to render
up his account.

Young's melodramatic account of the ecstasies and terrors
of the Last Judgment accepts the traditional view of hell as
a place of eternal torment. Johnson disapproved of Young's
subject since "the thought of the LAST DAY makes every
man more than poetical by spreading over his mind a general
obscurity of sacred horror, that oppresses distinction and dis-
dains expression." But he thought *The Last Day* had "an equa-
bility and propriety" which Young "afterwards either never
endeavoured or never attained."[16] There is no indication that
the mature Johnson disagreed with Young's view of hell. But
probably in Young and certainly in Johnson, there is a desire
to mitigate its terrors. In the seventeenth century, as D. P.

Walker has shown, the doctrine of eternal torment was subject to widespread reinterpretation, and a number of orthodox Anglicans in Johnson's century, his Oxford friend William Adams, for instance, rejected the traditional view. And it is worth noting that the Thirty-nine Articles "do not contain any affirmation of the eternity of hell" although the Forty-second Article of the 1552 prayer book had condemned "the dangerouse opinion that all menne, be thei never so ungodlie, shall at length be saved, when they have suffered pain for their sinnes a certain time appointed by God's justice."[17] Now Young puts a long speech into the mouth of a "damned soul" protesting the injustice of his fate. Young may well have sympathized privately with the argument of the damned soul, but as an orthodox Anglican it is unlikely he would have opposed the traditional view in print. As Walker points out, a major reason for the persistence of the doctrine was the widespread belief in its value as a deterrent, a belief which made people extremely reluctant to question it publicly.[18]

Whatever Johnson's opinion of hell's deterrent value, he was himself deterred from rejecting the traditional view by certain texts in the New Testament, especially by Christ's eschatological discourse in Matthew 25, a locus classicus for the belief in eternal torment and a difficult text for those who wished to mitigate the rigors of the traditional doctrine.[19] Johnson's favorable attitude toward the Roman Catholic doctrine of Purgatory indicates what he would like to have believed. There is "nothing unreasonable" in that doctrine since it assumes "that the generality of mankind are neither so obstinately wicked as to deserve everlasting punishment, nor so good as to merit being admitted into the society of the blessed spirits; and therefore . . . God is graciously pleased to allow of a middle state, where they may be purified by certain degrees of suffering." But Johnson could not get around the plain import of Matthew 25. A discussion with Boswell in 1777 indicates what I take to be his considered opinion on the matter. Boswell hopes certain scriptural texts "strong in support of the dreadful doctrine of an eternity of punishment" may admit of a figurative interpretation. Johnson is not sure they do, but he concedes that certain texts which are "strong" in favor of the doctrine "may admit of a mitigated interpretation." Boswell adds that Johnson talked "upon this awful and delicate question in a gentle tone, and as if afraid to be decisive."[20] Had Johnson summed up his opinion in the form of advice to a believer disturbed by this problem, he would have said, I think, something like this: Believe in whatever mitigations of the doctrine seem reasonable to you consistent with your interpretation of Matthew 25 and other "strong" texts, but *act* always as though the doctrine allowed of no mitigations whatever.

After this excursion into the area of Johnson's mature religious outlook, I return now to consider what the youthful Johnson would find in Sir Richard Blackmore's *Creation*. Johnson retained a lifelong esteem for this lengthy philosophical poem. Besides recommending Blackmore for inclusion in his *Lives of the Poets*, Johnson praised *Creation* as lacking "neither harmony of numbers, accuracy of thought, nor eloquence of diction." In *Creation* "truth is recommended by elegance, and elegance sustained by truth."[21] The inclusion of this poem in Johnson's Oxford library is our first indication of Johnson's acquaintance with the physico-theologians, a group of writers whose purpose it was, as Blackmore put it, to refute atheists and unbelievers by demonstrating "the existence of a God from the marks of wisdom, design, contrivance, and the choice of ends and means, which appear in the universe." What the mature Johnson thought of the argument from (or to) design, so popular in his century, we shall consider later; for the moment we may note that Blackmore is thorough. He proves the existence of God from "the structure and qualities of the earth and sea," from "the celestial motions," from "the several parts of the body of man," and from "the instincts in brute animals."[22] Johnson would find in *Creation* virtually all the arguments that occur again and again with little change as to basic assumptions and mode of reasoning from John Ray's *The Wisdom of God Manifested in the Works of Creation* (1691) down to William Paley's *Natural Theology; or Evidences of the Existence and*

Attributes of the Deity, collected from the Appearances of Nature (1802).

The early eighteenth century, in part as a reaction against the license of the Restoration era, saw the multiplication of religious societies "for deepening the devotional life and promoting the more frequent celebration of the Blessed Sacrament."[23] Robert Nelson, a wealthy and pious Anglican layman, threw himself into this work with great energy and devotion. His *Great Duty of Frequenting the Christian Sacrifice* is the expansion of an argument also stressed in his best known work, *A Companion for the Festivals and Fasts of the Church of England* (1703), which Johnson later praised as "a most valuable help to devotion" (II, 458). Johnson knew of Nelson's widespread reputation for piety and uprightness of life. He cites him in the *Adventurer* as an example of piety and learning without "the pride of singularity" and is reported to have believed that Richardson had Nelson in mind when forming the character of Sir Charles Grandison.[24] If Nelson practiced what he preached in the *Great Duty* and in his *Fasts and Festivals*, he would, like Johnson, have devoted particular parts of the day to private devotion and "exercises" of religion. There is extant a long letter of Nelson's, dated 1708, to a young cousin whose father was about to send the boy abroad to "breed" him to the business of the "Turkey" trade. Aside from attendance at all duly appointed public services of the Church, Nelson urges the boy "to live by rule and method; to divide the day into such proportions, that a proper time may be assigned for all your actions; that the hours of your devotion, of your business, and your diversions, may all be stated; thus time will not lie upon your hands, nor sting you with regret when past." Nelson insists upon frequent self-examination: "You must frequently examine yourself, that you may exercise repentance where you fall short of your duty, and that you may thank God where you have been enabled to perform it," and "the oftener you perform it, the less trouble and time it will take up; so that, if you would accustom yourself to recollection every evening before you say your prayers, you would easily know the state of your mind, by running over the actions of the day past; which would discover any false step that you have made, and which require a particular repentance."[25]

Now, I doubt that Johnson had any knowledge of Nelson's devotional practices. I cite Nelson here because there has been a tendency to assume that such practices were the exclusive property, so to speak, of Puritans and Evangelicals, or of those influenced by them. And so it has been thought that Johnson's similar devotional "exercises," as recorded in his *Diaries*, are best explained in terms of Puritan or Evangelical influence. But the kind of religious exercises which Nelson recommends to his young cousin are firmly grounded in Anglican tradition. So far as the eighteenth century is concerned, it should be remembered that the Evangelical movement was, after all, a religious *revival*, and if Wesley's group at Oxford in the 1730's stressed method and regularity in one's private devotions, they were merely following the recommendations of that Anglican High Churchman William Law,[26] and Law himself was recommending modes of private devotion older than Protestantism itself. Johnson's private devotions are a sign of religious *seriousness*, not an indication of Puritan or Evangelical influence or affinity.

Because the library he transported to Oxford contained few religious works, we may not assume that Johnson read slightly in religious literature before his Oxford residence. If it is true that he had "looked into a great many books," the laws of probability indicate that he must have dipped into a fair number of books on religious subjects. It is safe to say that most of the books he read came from his father's bookshop, to whose shelves he had unrestricted access, and the eighteenth-century bookseller, whatever his personal literary tastes, had to stock a far higher proportion of religious to secular works than his modern counterpart. The demand for religious works was great, especially before the rise of a novel-reading public had expanded the market for secular works.

Michael himself certainly had no objection to this state

of affairs. His own preference was for "sober works of instruction and piety." In 1706 he purchased the "great and
noble" library of the ninth Earl of Derby, a collection of
2900 volumes which included editions of "most of the Fathers
entire." One of Michael's sale catalogs survives in which
"small and common books" are slighted in favor of what the
prospective buyer would find "in the body of the catalog":
"law, mathematics, history; and for the learned in divinity,
there are Drs. South, Taylor, Tillotson, Beveridge, and Flavel,
etc, the best of that kind."[27] The first three of these eminent
seventeenth-century divines are often cited in Johnson's *Dictionary*; undoubtedly he made his first acquaintance with them
from his father's bookshelves.

I think we must assume, especially considering his reading habits—"being content to nibble whatever came his way
by chance," as Clifford puts it[28]—that by the time he entered
Oxford Johnson had acquired a broad, but desultory and un-
systematic acquaintance with many writers which those
"learned in divinity" would be expected to know.

But the collection of books he formed to take with him
to Oxford was a matter of deliberate choice, and insofar as
evidence of this sort is of weight, it reinforces the conclusion
that none of the religious works he had looked into had as
yet acted to stimulate that submerged religious feeling which
Sarah's instructional methods had done so much to repress.
This situation was to change dramatically during Johnson's
year at Oxford, but before turning to consider this period,
I wish to conclude this chapter with a final comment on the
matter of parental influence. There is no indication that Sarah's
piety, however narrow, was not thoroughly genuine, and sincerity is highly important in any transmission of influence
from parent to child. Insincerity is quickly detected; sincerity
makes an indelible impression. According to Gordon Allport,

> There is considerable evidence to show that the most
> religious minded adults were raised by parents who them-
> selves were deeply religious. It is not that children of
> pious parents always accept the doctrinal position in

which they were trained. Very often they rebel against parental orthodoxy, and yet the sincerity of their parents' outlook has profoundly influenced them. When their own worldly supports break down, they are more likely than not to find their parents' philosophy of life a desirable, though not necessarily a detailed, model to follow.[29]

Johnson's worldly supports were soon to break down; when they did, it was to the religion of his parents that he turned for support.

III

Oxford

JOHNSON WAS AT OXFORD for a little over thirteen months, from October 31, 1728, to December 12, 1729. This year marked a turning point in his religious life. Boswell tells us the story:

> While at Oxford, he took up Law's Call to the Unconverted, not with any serious intention but expecting to find it a dull book as such books generally are & perhaps to laugh at it. But he found Law quite an Overmatch for him; & this was the first occasion of his thinking earnestly of Religion, after he became capable of rational inquiry.[1]

It is interesting that Boswell—following Johnson's language? —misnames William Law's *Serious Call to a Devout and Holy Life* (1728). But "Call to the Unconverted" is an accurate statement of the book's intention. Although Law addresses himself not to unbelievers but to nominal Christians, he insists that such people are as much in need of conversion as "the rank heathendom which the early Church had to face."[2] From one point of view Law's book is simply the most eloquent of many a treatise exhorting nominal Christians to become Christians in very truth. Certainly, Law achieved his purpose with Johnson. As Gibbon remarked, "if Law finds a spark of piety in his reader's mind he will kindle it into flame." Johnson had that spark, and from this time on, as Clifford says, "he never deviated from his sturdy, if some-

times gloomy, acceptance of the truths of Christian faith."[3]
What sort of "conversion"—if that is the proper word—did
Johnson experience?

Two sorts of eighteenth-century attitudes toward conversion may be distinguished. The first is the Evangelical or
Wesleyan view; the second the view of those Anglicans un-
affected by, or opposed in varying degrees to, these religious
revivals. For reasons of economy, and because they are likely
to have more in common with Johnson so far as their views
on church organization and pastoral functions are concerned,
I confine myself for purposes of illustration to those Evangelicals not generally regarded as followers of Wesley—although a number of these men, like Johnson himself, had a
high personal regard for Wesley and his work. Both parties,
the Evangelicals and those outside the movement, agreed as
to the dangers of a mere nominal Christianity. Both agreed
that conversion was essential for salvation, and both could
accept Johnson's *Dictionary* definition of "conversion" as a
"change from reprobation to grace, from a bad life to a holy
life."

But they differed as to the way in which this change was
thought to be effected. In general, the Evangelicals believed
that conversion is a particular spiritual experience, occurring
at a definite moment in time. It might be instantaneous, or it
might occur in stages, so to speak, over a considerable period,
often with intervening moments of great spiritual anguish as
the believer found himself questioning whether the experience, often of shattering emotional intensity, was genuinely
"of God." Typically, the conversion begins with exposure
to a sermon, a religious exhortation, or a Biblical text, the
meaning of which suddenly strikes the believer with the force
of a revelation.

The case of the Rev. Richard Conyers provides a good
example of the instantaneous conversion:

His awakening was sudden. Having read Ephesians 3:8
in church as part of the lesson for the day, he realized
that the phrase 'the unsearchable riches of Christ' meant

nothing to him, and was plunged into despair. Light came to him on Christmas Day, 1758, from two verses, Hebrews 9:20: 'Without shedding of blood there is no remission,' and John 1:7: 'The blood of Jesus Christ his son cleanseth us from all sin.' He became so excited that he rushed about the house crying, 'I have found him, I have found him.'[4]

Other conversions were less ecstatic and more gradual, but in each case the believer could date the experience, he could describe it (often in detail), and the more ardent Evangelicals were convinced that only those who had experienced such a "felt" conversion were in a state of grace or on the way to it. A significant characteristic of the Evangelical conversion is that it involves an accession of saving spiritual *knowledge,* knowledge to be gained in no other way. The believer gains new insight into the nature of his particular relationship to Christ as Saviour, and this revelatory insight is a free gift of God or, more properly, of the third person of the Trinity. Again, the Evangelical conversion usually involves "a radical redirection of character,"[5] and this inward change often has striking external effects. Thus, after his conversion, John Berridge, one of the best known of the early Evangelicals, "destroyed all his old sermons and began preaching in an entirely new manner, often extempore. The effect was almost startling, and hearers began to flock to the church from all sides."[6]

Most Anglicans, however, seem to have thought of conversion as a process of gradual growth in Godliness extending over many years, perhaps over a lifetime. In his survey of Anglican devotional writing from the Reformation to the Oxford movement, C. J. Stranks distinguishes two attitudes toward conversion. Some Anglicans believe there must be

a radical redirection of character, a conscious dedication of all man's gifts and primary instincts to God, before the way of Christian edification can be effectively entered into. There must be, at some recognisable point of time, the deliberate choice of God and the repudiation of all that is contrary to him. To others the necessity for this one great experience is not so apparent. The choice and the dedication is a cumulative thing, proceeding over the years.[6a]

Anglicans could not deny the possibility of sudden conversions, but such experiences, especially if accompanied by striking outward effects, were widely distrusted in the eighteenth century as evidence of "enthusiasm" (defined in Johnson's *Dictionary* as "vain belief of private revelation; a vain confidence of divine favour or communication"). The reason for this distrust is historical, not theological. The Puritans, who had posed so great a danger to the Church, were widely considered to have been enthusiasts in religion, and many of them, like the Evangelicals, had preached the necessity of the sudden or "conscious" conversion. Distrust of the revivals as "Puritanism revived" lies behind Bishop Butler's rebuke to Wesley: "Sir, the pretending to extraordinary revelations and gifts of the Holy Ghost is a horrid thing—a very horrid thing," and the remark of Archbishop Drummond of York, who told Richard Conyers that "he would be better employed preaching the morality of Socrates than canting about the New Birth."[7]

Now it is true that Johnson's religious awakening has something in common with the Evangelical type of conversion experience. Boswell certainly thought it did. "This instance," he remarks,

> of a mind such as that of Johnson being first disposed, by an unexpected incident, to think with anxiety of the momentous concerns of eternity, and of 'what he should do to be saved,' may for ever be produced in opposition to the superficial and sometimes profane contempt that has been thrown upon those occasional impressions which it is certain many christians have experienced; though it must be acknowledged that weak minds, from an erroneous supposition that no man is in a state of grace who has not felt a particular conversion, have, in some cases, brought a degree of ridicule upon them; a ridicule, of

which it is inconsiderate or unfair to make a general application. (I, 69-70)

Some of the more ardent Evangelicals (Boswell's "weak minds") did indeed believe that "no man is in a state of grace who has not felt a particular conversion," and Johnson's experience is datable, and it was, in Boswell's language, an "occasional" impression. Moreover, Law's *Serious Call*, venerated by many Evangelicals, was a factor in the conversion of some of them. Reading the *Serious Call* in 1736, the Evangelical Thomas Adam

> realized the wide gulf between his own life and the ideal which Law set forth. For some ten years he continued in a state of uncertainty, almost of bewilderment, which grew so strong that he trembled and wept when taking the services, and even refrained from preaching. At last the dawn came, and the long darkness fled away. The means by which he came to see fresh light was St. Paul's Epistle to the Romans 1:6.[8]

But there is no indication that Johnson's encounter with the *Serious Call* was accompanied by the kind of spiritual experience which leads to the conviction that one is in a state of grace, nor did Johnson's encounter with Law bring him that inward peace, that conviction of being in harmony with God's purposes which is, again, a common feature of the Evangelical conversion. A major reason for distinguishing Johnson's experience from those of the Evangelical type is the mature Johnson's attitude toward what he calls "secret intimations of acceptance and forgiveness." Johnson cannot deny that some Christians have experienced such "intimations," but he is convinced that "these radiations of favour are not always felt by the sincerest penitents" and that for the vast majority of pious Christians, "nothing is granted in this world beyond rational *hope*; and with *hope* founded on *promise*, we may well be satisfied" (III, 295 n.1). This is hardly the language of a man who has himself experienced "fresh light" through a particular spiritual experience. Again, the Evangelical conversion brought with it such confidence in the

truths of religion that the Evangelicals were not interested in
that much-discussed question, the matter of the "Christian
evidences." Because they were uninterested in "proving" what
to them was self-evident, "the Evangelicals produced no works
in the defense of the Christian faith." But Johnson's encounter
with Law had no such effect. S. G. Brown speaks rightly of
Johnson's "unending quest for . . . evidences of the truth of
Christianity."[9] Like Thomas Adam, Johnson "realized the
wide gulf between his own life and the ideal which Law set
forth," but whereas the *Serious Call* merely helped to pre-
pare Adam for the "fresh light" he received years later, there
is no indication that Johnson's reading of the book was accompanied, or followed, by the kind of revelatory insight which
Adam received from Romans 1:6. And the *Serious Call* has
nothing itself to say about the nature of the conversion process.
Law sets forth no theory of conversion, "particular" or otherwise. Law is concerned simply to show that the gospels enjoin
a certain way of life. For Law in the *Serious Call* the unconverted are those who reject his "call"; the converted are
those who try to live by his precepts. There must be a conversion certainly, a deliberate turning to God, but Law is not
interested in the way his logic and eloquence may affect
individual readers. If they reform their lives, that is enough
for him, whatever the nature of the process which leads to
this reformation.

Without attempting, then, to associate Johnson's conversion with the spiritual fervors and exaltations of the Evangelical religious awakening, or with the acquisition on his
part of any particular revelatory insight into the nature of his
relationship with God, we need not deny that the *Serious Call*
had a powerful emotional effect upon him. His term "overmatch" seems to indicate as much. Law's eloquence over-
powered and convinced him: he would become a Christian
in very truth. That he immediately attempted to reform his
life in accord with Law's teaching seems clear if his memoran-
dum of October 1729 was written after he had read the
Serious Call: "I bid farewell to Sloth, being resolved hence-
forth not to listen to her siren strains" (*Works*, I, 26).

But it is here that the *Serious Call* proved an overmatch for Johnson in a very different sense. Law's book differs from many another work of similar intention in the strictness of its precepts. Law has an ideal—the ideal of Christian perfection —which is extremely rigorous, extremely ascetic, and quite impossible for ordinary human flesh to live up to. As Miss Balderston says, "what Law actually demands of all Christians is saintliness." Law could state the ideal of Christian perfection with moving eloquence and sincerity because he came very near achieving it in his own life. An ethic of asceticism, renunciation, and self-denial was easy for Law, it came naturally to him, and he could never understand why it should not be as easy and as delightful for others as for him. It was only necessary to point the way. "One single thought," he tells us, "upon the happiness this [ideal of Christian perfection] leads to is sufficient to make all people saints."[10]

If we consider the matter from the point of view only of Johnson's ease and comfort, it was an unlucky accident that put Law's book into his hands. Here was a young man of a powerful and inquiring mind, eager to learn all he could about the things of this world, painfully conscious of his poverty and physical handicaps, but fiercely proud, and determined that the world should take notice of him. And from Law he learns that worldly ambitions are mere dross, and not dross merely, but active impediments to the Christian life. Law does not demand withdrawal from the world, but he does insist on carrying the ethic of renunciation *into* the world.

Just how far the mature Johnson was affected by this aspect of Law's teaching is a question. As against what Professor Quinlan rightly calls the "ascetic streak" in Johnson,[11] there is Johnson's praise of "luxury," his condemnation of those who withdraw from the world without very good reason, and the difficulty of deciding whether, or how far, Johnson condemned himself for engaging in worldly activities and pleasures difficult to reconcile with Law's teaching. But it may well be that in his first flush of enthusiasm for the *Serious Call*, Johnson was bothered not only by his indulgence in particular vices condemned by Law (sloth), but by his realization of the wide discrepancy between his own goals in life, his own ambitions, and Law's rejection of such secular preoccupations.

At any rate, there is reason to believe that the immediate effect of the *Serious Call* upon Johnson, far from producing in him that kind of spiritual illumination which brings peace and comfort, was actually a source of misery as Johnson tried, but failed, to live up to the high ideal of the Christian life that Law set before him. Miss Balderston believes Johnson's failure to live up to Law's conception of the Christian life "was at least a contributing cause of the serious attack of depression which began in December 1729 and which, along with his lack of money, forced him to leave Oxford without his degree, after only thirteen months of residence."[12]

In evaluating the immediate impact of the *Serious Call* upon Johnson, one must keep in mind two dates, Johnson's twentieth (1729-30) and twenty-second (1731-32) years, both of which he mentions as marking periods of crisis in his life. In both instances the crisis was marked by a severe attack of melancholia, that disease which afflicted Johnson off and on for the rest of his life. Johnson's twentieth year marks the period of his encounter with the *Serious Call* (he may actually have read the book before his twentieth birthday) and the attack of melancholia mentioned by Miss Balderston. But, as we have seen, he also tells us that he had been totally regardless of religion from the age of ten "till two and twenty." And here there is no mention of Law; it is "sickness" which brings religion back to him. It is true that Johnson says "*I think* from ten till two and twenty" (my italics). It might be thought he was mistaken and should have said "from ten till twenty," but his twenty-second year seems to have established itself rather firmly in his own mind and in that of his friends as a time of crisis. He told Boswell that he once walked a good deal but "left it off at two and twenty" when he "grew melancholy," and his friend George Steevens speaks confidently of "that insanity" which Johnson "from his two and twentieth year . . . had taught himself to apprehend."[13]

There is no question about the earlier attack. As the

first affliction of this sort it was especially frightening and, as Johnson told Boswell, he did not then know how to manage it. He feared he was losing his mind and may even have "entertained thoughts of suicide." Writing of this period much later Johnson remarked that his health had been, from his twentieth year, such as had seldom afforded him "a single day of ease."[14] But there is no reason why one attack, having run its course, should not have been followed, a year or so later, by another. The years 1730-34, years of "dejection and indolence," as Clifford calls them, form one of the unhappiest periods of Johnson's life as he struggled to establish himself in the distasteful profession of a schoolmaster.

In any case it seems wise, in view of Johnson's statements, to avoid too strict a cause-and-effect concept of the relationship between the *Serious Call* and Johnson's melancholia. Moreover, if Johnson seriously entertained thoughts of suicide during his twentieth year, one must assume that this first attack plunged him into such depths of despair that the teachings of religion could hardly prevail against it, or that his commitment to those teachings was not as firm, in spite of Law, as it later became. My own view is that Johnson experienced a period of religious crisis extending over two or three years, and while I think the encounter with the *Serious Call* marked a very real conversion in the sense of a definite "turning" toward religion, it may well be that Johnson, looking back on this period many years later, thought of this encounter as a beginning, a rediscovery leading toward the firmer commitment to religion which is implied in the statement that sickness brought it back to him—some two years after he had read Law's book. After all, he does say, not that the *Serious Call* brought religion back to him, but merely that it started him "thinking earnestly" of it.

Sickness, then, is probably to be given equal weight with the eloquence of Law as a factor in Johnson's rediscovery of religion. In later life he never denied that illness and the fear of death are powerful incentives to a serious consideration of Christian teaching on the subject of "futurity." So far as his melancholia is concerned, fears of death, and worse, fears of insanity, would certainly have caused him to think seriously of these teachings even if he had never heard of Law's book. And his worldly supports had indeed broken down. The loss of his hopes for a degree was a heavy blow to his youthful ambition because a university degree was highly desirable, if not absolutely necessary, for any profession likely to appeal to him.

We cannot probe the recesses of Johnson's mind and heart. But so far as external factors are concerned, along with the eloquence of Law, we must consider Johnson's illness, his fears of death or insanity, and the apparent collapse of his worldly prospects as powerful motives for his commitment to the religion of his parents, with its promise of eternal happiness—the "great article" of Christianity as Johnson later called it (III, 188)—whatever the miseries and frustrations of this earthly existence.

Johnson said the *Serious Call* first started him thinking earnestly of religion after he became capable of "rational inquiry." And it is clear that Johnson's religious awakening involved not only an attempt to reform his life in accord with Law's principles but an active inquiry into the public role of Christianity as an institution, as a powerful force in the realm of politics and international affairs. He was interested not only in the subjective aspect of religion but in its objective aspect as a social force affecting the destinies of nations. This point leads us to a consideration of another work Johnson read at Oxford, the Portuguese Jesuit Jeronymo Lobo's account of his voyage to Abyssinia, as translated by the French Catholic Oratorian Joachim Le Grand, and published in 1728 as *Voyage Historique d'Abissinie du R. P. Jerome Lobo*.

Following his departure from Oxford Johnson spent some time in Birmingham on a visit to his friend Edmund Hector. One day when dining with the Birmingham bookseller Thomas Warren, Johnson mentioned that he had read the Lobo book at Oxford, and that he wondered whether a translation and abridgment might not prove a profitable undertaking. Urged to undertake it himself, Johnson worked more or less steadily on the book during the winter of 1733-34, and Warren published it the following year.

At first sight, as Donald Greene has said, this seems a curious choice for a fledgling author, "this abridgement and translation into English of a French version of a Portuguese Jesuit's account of his experiences in Abyssinia in the early seventeenth century."[15] To be sure, Johnson to the end of his days manifested an active curiosity with regard to the customs and manners of far-off lands little known to the average Englishman. As he says in the dedication to the Lobo book, "A generous and elevated mind is distinguished by nothing more certainly than an eminent degree of curiosity; nor is that curiosity ever more agreeably or usefully employed than in examining the laws and customs of foreign nations." Until quite recently it was assumed that Johnson valued Lobo chiefly for his accuracy as a reporter: Lobo "has amused his readers with no romantick absurdities or incredible fictions."[16] But I think Johnson was primarily interested in the religious content of the Lobo-Le Grand volume.

In the first place, it is clear from his preface that he had read other works dealing largely with Abyssinian religion, either before or after his encounter with Lobo. One was the *Church-History of Abyssinia* (1696) by the Rev. Michael Geddes; the other the *Historia Aethiopica* (1681) by the German Lutheran scholar Job Ludolf.

The Lobo book itself had a certain topical interest. The French translator Le Grand looks askance at Portuguese missionary methods, and since the alliance with Portugal was one of the keystones of Whig policy it may be that Johnson and Warren thought the book might have particular appeal to Tory readers. But they probably hoped that Protestant Englishmen of every political persuasion might take an interest in a book which appeared as the latest, most up-to-date document in a Catholic-Protestant controversy of long-standing continuance.

Before giving an account of this controversy it will be well to give the reader some idea of the makeup of Johnson's book. Johnson's version of Lobo-Le Grand may be divided into two parts, the first consisting of Lobo's "Voyage," his "Description of Abyssinia," and a "Continuation of the History of Abyssinia down to the Beginning of the Eighteenth Century" by Le Grand himself. The second part consists of Le Grand's "Dissertations on the History, Antiquities, Government, Religion, Manners and natural History of Abyssinia." Now of Le Grand's sixteen dissertations, the first and the last eight, over half the total number, are concerned with Abyssinian religion and with the Catholic-Protestant controversy mentioned above. There is in fact much more of Le Grand (252 pages) than of Lobo (144 pages) in Johnson's book. It is clear from Le Grand's "Continuation" and from his elaborate dissertations that he intended his book to be not merely a translation of Lobo but a compendium of extant knowledge about Abyssinia, superseding all earlier books on the subject. And it is clear as well that he conceives it a major part of his task to support the Catholic interpretation of Abyssinian Christianity as against the Protestant view, as set forth in particular by Job Ludolf in his *Historia Aethiopica.*

Now let us look at Johnson's preface more closely. Of eleven paragraphs commenting specifically on the content of the Lobo-Le Grand volume, three extol Lobo's accuracy as a reporter. Of the remaining eight paragraphs, which constitute the body of the preface, seven have to do with religion. The other comments on Le Grand's "discourses on indifferent [i.e., non-religious] subjects," and here Johnson is content to remark simply that these "will divert, as well as instruct" the reader. Thus, of these eleven paragraphs, four comment on secular matters as against seven on religion, and these last are, on the average, somewhat longer. And it is only with Le Grand's dissertations that Johnson attempted "an exact translation." It seems clear, at the very least, that Johnson thought the religious content of the book a major drawing card in attracting readers.

I turn now to the religious controversy itself. It concerns the Catholic-Protestant debate as to the nature of the primitive, apostolic church. The Catholics argued that the primitive church was truly "Catholic" and that the Protestants, abjuring Catholicism at the Reformation, had thereby cut themselves loose from the true Christian and apostolic tradition. The Protestants, on the other hand, saw themselves as reformers, and the Protestant religion as a return, so far as this was possible, to the pure faith of the primitive church before the abuses and corruptions introduced by Rome. As the Portuguese, actuated by commercial and imperial ambition, moved into Abyssinia, and as more was learned of the religion of the Abyssinians, it became apparent that here was yet another form of Christianity, also claiming direct descent from the primitive, apostolic church. The fact that the Abyssinians claimed to be authentic Christians posed a problem for the Portuguese. An independent Abyssinian Church posed too great a threat to Portuguese imperialistic ambition to be easily tolerated, but if the Abyssinians were Christians indeed, what could be done about it? Lobo indicates how the Portuguese solved their problem. So many errors had been introduced into Abyssinian religion that, according to Lobo, "their present Religion, is nothing but a kind of confused Miscellany of Jewish and Mahometan Superstitions, with which they have corrupted those Remnants of Christianity which they still retain." Hence Lobo can proceed on his mission of conversion with a good conscience: "To bring back this People into the Enclosure of the Catholick Church, from which they had been separated so many Ages, was the sole view and intention, with which we undertook so long and toilsome a Journey."[17]

It was thus in the interest of the Portuguese to stress the differences between Abyssinian and Catholic Christianity, but in so doing they provided a convenient target for Protestant attack. The most formidable and the best known of these attacks was that of Ludolf in his *Historia Aethiopica*. Taking advantage of the Portuguese stress on the differences between Abyssinian and Catholic Christianity, Ludolf finds the difference to lie in the fact that Abyssinian Christianity is actually much nearer to Protestant than to Catholic Christianity. Vigorously combating the Portuguese contention that the

Abyssinian church represented a debased, Judaized form of Christianity, Ludolf finds "striking parallels between the Abyssinian practices, admittedly going back to very ancient times, and modern Protestantism, thus supporting the Protestant position that the reformed churches were a return to the Christianity of the apostolic age before the abuses introduced by Rome."[18]

It is the main purpose of Le Grand to refute this contention. His first dissertation "Upon Mr. Ludolf's History of Abyssinia" indicates the polemical character of what follows, and his remark that Ludolf *"ne trouve rien de mal parmi les Abissins que ce qu'ils ont de commun avec l'Eglise Catholique"*[19] is not an unfair summary of Ludolf's own polemical stance. Le Grand, then, attempts to refute Ludolf by stressing parallels between Abyssinian religious beliefs and practices and those of contemporary Catholicism. At the same time Le Grand is unsympathetic to the Portuguese Jesuits. Since he believes their methods of dealing with the Abyssinians crass, if not barbarous, and hence deserving of failure, it is no concern of his that his argument undercuts their excuse for attempting to convert the Abyssinians to Catholicism. Le Grand's attitude toward the Portuguese Jesuits is summed up in his remark that they were "men zealous indeed, but too much prejudiced, and who had little other Knowledge than the Learning of their Schools."[20] As Le Grand sees it, they were not fitted by temperament or education for the momentous task they had undertaken.

As Donald Greene has said, Johnson in his preface moderates among the disputants—Lobo, Ludolf, and Le Grand— with an appearance of "judicious detachment."[21] Johnson sums up the controversy as follows:

> If the Portuguese were biassed by any particular views, another bias equally powerful may have deflected the Frenchman from the truth; for they evidently write with contrary designs: the Portuguese, to make their mission seem more necessary, endeavoured to place, in the strongest light, the differences between the Abyssinian and

Roman church; but the great Ludolfus, laying hold on the advantage, reduced these later writers to prove their conformity. (Preface, pp. 257-58.)

And Johnson, as Greene says, concludes with this strongly Protestant and "above-the-battle" judgment: "Upon the whole, the controversy seems of no great importance to those who believe the holy Scriptures sufficient to teach the way of salvation; but, of whatever moment it may be thought, there are no proofs sufficient to decide it."

It is true, as we shall see, that Johnson's interest in the religious content of the Lobo-Le Grand volume has another, and a more significant, focus. But it is not true that Johnson took little or no interest in the controversy. He was not as detached as the tone of his preface implies. In the preface, while he admits that the Portuguese were biased, he has qualified praise for Lobo who, he tells us, "neither exaggerates overmuch the merits of the Jesuits" nor "aggravates" unduly "the vices of the Abyssinians." One would gather from such a remark that Johnson's own translation would be reasonably objective. Yet this is not the case. Joel J. Gold has shown that Johnson slanted his material, often through significant omissions, in such a way that Lobo and the Portuguese missionary enterprise often appear in a more unfavorable light than they do in Le Grand's account: "By deemphasizing the Roman Catholic and Jesuit claims of belonging to the true 'Apostolic' church and of interpreting the word of God, Johnson sharply limits the authority they can muster to support their campaign against the Abyssinians."[22] It is clear that Johnson took a personal and partisan interest in the controversy, so much so that it is hard to acquit him of a practice that, today at least, would be considered distinctly unethical.

Nevertheless, it is true that for Johnson the controversy per se is of much less importance than another consideration. If he slants his material against the Portuguese, he does so out of a burning sense of indignation against what he considers the sanguinary, persecuting spirit of the Portuguese missionary enterprise in particular and of the Roman Catholic church in general. Not all of Johnson's preface breathes a spirit of judicious detachment. After praising Le Grand for having dared in the midst of Catholic France "to declare his disapprobation" of the Portuguese patriarch Oviedo's "sanguinary zeal," he remarks "with how little reason" the Portuguese Jesuits "profess themselves the followers of JESUS, who left this great characteristick to his disciples, that they should be known by loving one another, by universal and unbounded charity and benevolence." And the next paragraph, as Donald Greene has said (*Politics*, p. 68), constitutes a tremendous denunciation of the Roman Catholic church generally. It is by far the most eloquent paragraph in the preface, and one of the most eloquent in the whole body of Johnson's writings:

> Let us suppose an inhabitant of some remote and superior region, yet unskilled in the ways of men, having read and considered the precepts of the gospel, and the example of our Saviour, to come down in search of the true church. If he would not inquire after it among the cruel, the insolent, and the oppressive; among those who are continually grasping at dominion over souls as well as bodies; among those who are employed in procuring to themselves impunity for the most enormous villainies, and studying methods of destroying their fellow creatures, not for their crimes, but their errours; if he would not expect to meet benevolence engaged in massacres, or to find mercy in a court of inquisition—he would not look for the true church in the church of Rome.

"Not for their crimes, but their errours." Nowhere in his translation does Johnson attack Roman Catholic doctrine. Indeed there were few eighteenth-century Protestants who looked with a kindlier eye upon this body of doctrine than Johnson in the years of his maturity. Denouncing the Catholics for their crimes against the spirit of Christian charity, this paragraph is not inconsistent with Johnson's later pronouncements in defense of certain Catholic doctrinal positions. Nevertheless, insofar as it constitutes a fervent and unqualified denunciation of a Christian denomination as a whole, it is, I believe, unique. It reflects all the generous idealism of the youthful "convert"—and youth's immoderation as well.

What, we may ask at this point, had Johnson learned from the earnest thinking about religion which his encounter with Law's *Serious Call* had inspired him to undertake? What conclusions had he reached? There is, first of all, the thoroughly Protestant conviction concerning the gospels as "sufficient to teach the way of Salvation." More significant is the way Johnson interprets the spirit and message of the New Testament. If for Johnson, as for Law, points of doctrine fade in importance before the sine qua non of Christian charity, it may be presumed that both men distinguish this sort of charity from other, non-Christian sorts. Johnson's definition of this virtue as "universal and unbounded charity and benevolence" strongly recalls Law's emphasis throughout the *Serious Call*, and Johnson, like Law, always thought of it as a religious obligation rather than a tendency more or less natural to unregenerate human nature. As Law has it, "By love, I do not mean any natural tenderness, which is more or less in people, according to their constitutions; but I mean a larger principle of the soul, founded in reason and piety, which makes us tender, kind, and benevolent to all our fellow creatures, as creatures of God, and for His sake."[23]

Johnson agreed. Moreover, I believe Johnson had already come to the conclusion which he expressed in later life that charity, as understood by Christians, was brought into the world by revelation: the ancients, knowing and practicing the virtues of temperance, fortitude, justice, and the like, knew nothing of charity as Christians understand it. Thus in his edition of Shakespeare, Johnson gives us the lines where Edgar in *King Lear* says to his dying brother, "Let's exchange charity,/ I am no less in blood than thou art, Edmund" (V, iii, 166), and comments, believing the word "charity" anachronistic in a pagan society: "Our author by negligence gives his heathens the sentiments and practices of christianity. In *Hamlet* there is the same solemn act of final reconciliation, but with exact propriety, for the personages are Christians."

Commenting on John 13:34-35, Law had remarked that

the newness of this precept did not consist in this, that men were commanded to love one another; for this was an old precept, both of the law of Moses, and of nature. But it was new in this respect, that it was to imitate a new, and till then unheard-of example of love; it was to love one another, as Christ had loved us.

And if men are to know that we are disciples of Christ, by thus loving one another, according to His new example of love, then it is certain that if we are void of this love, we make it as plainly known unto men, that we are none of His disciples.[24]

And this, of course, was what the Portuguese Jesuits had done. They had made it known among men by their crimes against Christian charity that they were "none of His disciples." And thus, although both the Protestant Geddes and the Catholic Le Grand agree that the Abyssinians were guilty of a rather serious heresy, "holding that there is but one Nature in Christ, which is the Divine, by which they will have the Humane to be swallowed up,"[25] Johnson in his anger at the sanguinary zeal of the Jesuits, presents the Abyssinians, not as "heretics or schismatics," but as the innocent victims of Portuguese aggression who rightly wish "to hold fast to the faith of their ancestors."[26]

We see, then, that Johnson did take a lively personal interest in the religious content of the Lobo-Le Grand volume, and we have seen something of the nature and direction of this interest. Johnson's evaluation of the various parties to the dispute on the basis of their display of Christian charity breathes the very spirit of William Law's *Serious Call*. What is evident also—and this seems less characteristic of Law—is the wide-ranging curiosity of Johnson's mind.

Although Le Grand writes as a liberal Catholic of the early eighteenth century, his dissertations are formidably learned in the seventeenth-century manner. There is much lengthy quotation of "authorities," ancient and modern. Johnson as translator shows himself fully in command of this material. He fulfills his promise of exactness in the sense of preserving always the tenor of Le Grand's argument but he never hesitates to reduce and to simplify the apparatus of Le Grand's scholarship. Le Grand's lengthy "proof texts" from the Church

Fathers and other authorities are sometimes reduced to a citation, sometimes summarized in a sentence or two. Here Johnson acts as modernizer, adapting the cumbrous apparatus of seventeenth-century scholarly style to the requirements of a new age.

Aside from Johnson's hope that his translation would bring him some much-needed money, I think we must assume a lively curiosity on his part concerning the history and doctrines of Abyssinian Christianity. I think he had already acquired a rather thorough knowledge of ecclesiastical history, both Catholic and Protestant, and of the major heresies and theological conflicts that form so important a part of that history. He already had all the "facts," as he might have said, and he probably acquired most of them during that period of hard reading preceding his Oxford residence when, as he tells us, he looked into a great many books quite unknown to the average undergraduate. Already conversant with the history of European Christianity in both its major branches, his curiosity was aroused by what had been learned concerning yet a third branch of Christianity, unfamiliar to most Europeans but possibly quite as authentic a branch of the historic faith as the European varieties. It seems clear from his mention of Geddes and Ludolf that Johnson had made a special study of Abyssinian Christianity, and it is quite likely that he had read other books on the subject which he had no occasion to mention in his preface.[27]

And so, along with Johnson's effort to reform his life in accord with Law's principles, there is the fact of Johnson's insatiable curiosity. Johnson wants to become a Christian, but he wants, as part and parcel of that becoming, to know what there is to know about Christianity in all its branches from apostolic times to the eighteenth century. This is a part of what being "in earnest" about religion means for Johnson.

Johnson, of course, held the orthodox view that the essentials of Christianity are few and simple: the illiterate peasant is quite as well off so far as prospective salvation is concerned as the most learned bishop in the land. But in the New Testament parable of the talents Johnson found a religious commandment which seemed to him of the utmost importance. As Johnson sees it, God demands that every man employ to the fullest those talents with which he has been endowed. This applies to every activity, religious or secular, provided the secular activity violates no dictate of religion and is of benefit to man (dictionary-making, for instance). If, by education and mental equipment, a man is able to give reasons why he is an Anglican rather than a Presbyterian or a deist, he has a religious obligation to acquire the knowledge which will enable him to do so. The more he learns about his religion, up to the limit of his abilities, the more acceptable he is in the sight of God, and the only way to know one's own religion in depth is to know how it differs from others.[28]

Many years after the period I am concerned with here, Johnson and Boswell discussed the question of subscription to the Thirty-nine Articles as a requirement for entrance into the universities. Johnson admitted that subscription was "making boys at the University subscribe to what they do not understand." But he believed that since the universities were founded to bring up "members for the Church of England," some kind of subscription, indicating adherence to that church, was necessary, and that it might as well be subscription to the Articles since a simple oath indicating adherence to the Church of England would entail the same difficulty:

> for still the young men would be subscribing to what they do not understand. For if you should ask them, what do you mean by the Church of England? Do you know in what it differs from the Presbyterian Church? from the Romish Church? from the Greek Church? from the Coptic Church? they could not tell you. So, Sir, it comes to the same thing. (II, 151)

But Samuel Johnson was not one of these ignorant young men. By his middle twenties he knew a great deal about these differences, and would probably have considered himself culpably negligent had he not known of them.

Johnson's Correspondence with Hill Boothby

JOHNSON'S PREFACE to the Lobo-Le Grand volume and Law's *Serious Call* are both written within the spirit of an Anglican tradition, always powerful, but perhaps especially so in the late seventeenth and early eighteenth centuries—a tradition which avoids theological controversy in favor of a broadly based irenical approach to religion. Johnson's very real interest in theology and theological controversy should not obscure the fact that Johnson has a system of priorities to which he always adhered. Controversy is inevitable in a religion such as Christianity where doctrine is important—and Johnson never denies the importance of correct belief—but granted a knowledge of the few beliefs necessary for salvation, conduct is always more important than one's exact position on doctrinal points. This is the attitude of most eighteenth-century Englishmen, ever mindful of the fact that their forefathers had gone to war over matters of doctrine and church government. As we have seen, Johnson's indignation at the idea of persecuting men, not for their crimes but for their errors of doctrine, is an important key to our understanding of his Lobo translation.

Nevertheless, the growing strength of the Evangelical movement within the Church of England forced attention to doctrinal matters. The Evangelicals insisted upon their orthodoxy, but it was clear that their interpretation of the

Thirty-nine Articles differed—or seemed to differ—from that of many Anglicans.

Perhaps because Boswell in the *Life* printed only one letter of Johnson's to the latter's beloved Hill Boothby, the Johnson-Boothby correspondence, which extended over a period of nearly two-and-a-half years, is not as well known as it should be. This correspondence is interesting chiefly as indicating the mature Johnson's attitude—he was then in his mid-forties—toward that religious movement known as the Evangelical Revival.

Something must be said of Hill Boothby herself. Johnson met her in 1739 while on a visit to John Taylor at Ashbourne. He also met her dearest friend Mary Meynell, and a neighbor, William Fitzherbert, whom Johnson later described as "a gay good humoured fellow, generous of his money and his meat, and desirous of nothing but cheerful society among people distinguished in *some* way, in *any* way, I think."[1] In 1744 Mary married William. After bearing him six children, Mary died in the spring of 1753, naming Miss Boothby (now forty-five, one year Johnson's senior) "her sole executor and residuary legatee."[2] From this time until her death in January 1756 Hill Boothby was a member of the Fitzherbert family, devoting herself to the care of Fitzherbert's motherless children.

It is at this point, a few months after Mary's death, that Johnson requested the favor of a regular correspondence with Miss Boothby. His own wife had died in 1752; roughly three months before the initiation of the correspondence with Miss Boothby he noted in his diary his intention "to seek a new wife."[3] Miss Boothby was, I think, a more likely candidate than most. At any rate, there is no question of his devotion to her. This fact gives the correspondence a particular interest, since if there was any one person at this period in Johnson's life who could have wrought a change in his religious opinions, Hill Boothby is that person. Joseph Baretti believed that "had she lived some years longer Johnson would in all probability have become quite an enthusiast in point of religion, and have gone mad with it. He was so strongly inclined to it."[4]

It is clear at least that Miss Boothby, like her dear friend Mary Meynell, was a woman of unusual piety. And the problems she faced on becoming a member of Fitzherbert's household were the same the pious Mary had encountered. To the worldly good-natured Fitzherbert, at whose table "Rousseau and St. Austin would have been equally welcome," Mary opposed, as Johnson put it, "another way of thinking; her first care was to preserve her husband's soul from corruption; her second, to keep his estate entire for their children." And Johnson believed he owed his good reception in the family to Mary's idea that he set a good example for Fitzherbert and his guests, who would not swear or take other "conversation-liberties" in his presence. Johnson makes it clear that the easy-going Fitzherbert was restive in the face of Mary's strict piety, and that when she died he "felt at once afflicted and released."[5]

If Mary's first care was to preserve her husband's soul from corruption, Miss Boothby's first care was to do the same for Mary's children. Regarding Fitzherbert's way of life as worldly and frivolous, she did her best to preserve the children from its contaminating influence. But her task was more difficult than Mary's since she lacked the status and authority of a wife. At the same time the children were noisy, she was in ill health, and had, in addition, the management of a large household. One may easily forget the long hours and sheer domestic drudgery to which even gentlewomen in the eighteenth century were exposed. Her letters to Johnson are full of apologies for not writing oftener; her excuse is that she had little time to herself. One is not surprised to find that Johnson, who hated solitude, could not fully appreciate her position. "You do not pity me," she writes,

> when I am whirled round by a succession of company; yet you are anxious for my health. Now this is, though perhaps unknown to you, really a contradiction. For one day's crowd, with the preceding necessary preparations to receive them, the *honours*, as it is called, of a large table, with the noise, &c. attending, pulls down my feeble frame more than anything you can imagine.

And she goes on to complain that for some time past she has seldom had "one half hour in a day" to herself.[6]

For a glimpse at what these "necessary preparations" involved, we may note the time when Fitzherbert "and his company"

> arrived here on Thursday last, all at a loss what to do with themselves in *still life*. They set out yesterday to Derby race, and return on Friday, with some forty more people, to eat a turtle; weight, an hundred and thirty. This feast, I, who, you know, love eating, am preparing for them. It will be a day of fatigue. (pp. 113-14)

We need not exaggerate her plight. She was no mere upper servant; she had social position and her own friends outside Fitzherbert's circle. Fitzherbert traveled a good deal, and more often than not she enjoyed traveling, believing it improved her health. And so far as the children are concerned, her letters record one signal triumph. She was the prime mover in having Fitzherbert's son and heir sent away to school at the tender age of six. "A fine lively boy," she informed Johnson, "but, *entre nous*, too indulgent a father will make it necessary for him to be sent to school; the sooner the better" (pp. 56-57). And sent he was. And there is no doubt of her genuine love for her "jewels," the children. There were, after all, intervals of quiet when she was left to her own devices and could enjoy the company of her favorite child, the precocious "Miss Fitzherbert" (a girl of nine), who was studying the "Ramblers" to form her style and hoped to send Johnson a specimen of her abilities (p. 97).

Nevertheless, one suspects there were times when Hill Boothby would have liked nothing better than to have retired from the "world" altogether; that she would have found in a household like that of William Law at King's Cliffe just the sort of environment that would have suited her particular brand of piety and her longing for peace and quiet. This was partly the natural result of her difficult situation, but it was also the result of religious convictions formed years earlier, although her trials as mistress of Fitzherbert's household may well have strengthened her reliance upon heavenly rather than earthly comforts. She was pulled two ways. Regarding her care of the children as a sacred trust, she was drawn into the world and its problems, but her religious convictions were such that she could never regard the "worldly" life she was forced to lead with anything but distaste. As a result, there is a constant tension in her letters between what may be described as attitudes of submission to the world and its problems, and of resignation, withdrawal, or "letting go." After agreeing with Johnson that this or that social duty is important, she will often add a phrase expressing her resignation to the will of God. Agreeing with Johnson as to the importance of having the children properly educated, she adds, "I will labour all I can to produce plenty. But sanguine hopes will never tempt me to feel the torture of cutting disappointment. I have seen even Pauls plant, and Apollos water in vain, and am convinced God only can give the increase" (p. 56). An attitude expressed repeatedly in her letters is summed up in her remark that the text "*sufficient unto the day, is the evil thereof*" is her "Preservative from all anxious thought for the morrow." She looks "not forward but to an eternity of peace and joy, and in this view all VAIN solicitude for the things of this life is taken away" (p. 50).

Such an attitude is not uncommon among pious Christians and is certainly not distinctively "evangelical." But what is important for our purposes is that Johnson was disturbed by it. Ever mindful of the parable of the talents, and with his strong sense of social obligation, Johnson believed that one earned one's salvation in the dust and heat of this world; one put one's talents to use as best one could in the ordinary duties of "common life." Believing this, he believed Hill Boothby carried her principle of resignation too far, so far that she was sometimes inclined to neglect such duties. Many years after Miss Boothby's death, Johnson told Mrs. Thrale that the lady had "somewhat disqualified herself for the duties of *this* life, by her perpetual aspirations after the *next*."[7] Baretti might have replied that Johnson was able to take this detached view only because he was now no longer under her influence. But

the correspondence indicates quite clearly that this was precisely what Johnson believed at the time—and he did not
hesitate to voice his opinion. He accused her of being too
"abstracted from common life," and she admitted the charge:

> It is true, I am abstracted from common life, as you say.
> What is common life, but a repetition of the same things
> over and over? And is it made up of such things, as a
> thinking, reflecting being can bear the repetition of, over
> and over without weariness? I have found not; and there-
> fore my view is turned to the things of that life which
> must be begun here, is ever new and increasing, and will
> be continued eternally hereafter. Yet, mistake me not, I
> am so far from excluding social duties from this life, that
> I am sure they are a part of it, and can only be duly and
> truly exerted in it. Common life, I call not social life; but,
> in general, that dissipation and wandering which leads
> from the duties of it. While I was in town, I did not feel
> myself as a part of that multitude around me. The objects
> I saw at dinners, &c. *except yourself,* when they had any
> of my attention, drew it only to pity their want of at-
> tention to what chiefly concerned their happiness; and
> oftener they were as passing straws on the surface of a
> Dovedale stream, and went as lightly and as quick, over
> the surface of my mind. (pp. 93-95)

The condemnation of ordinary social pleasures as frivolous and distracting, so evident in this letter, is present
throughout Miss Boothby's part of the correspondence. Here
we approach an attitude which, although again not distinctively evangelical, is rightly considered a concomitant of the
stricter piety which that movement encouraged. William Law,
whose condemnation of worldly pleasures Evangelicals found
highly congenial, wrote a treatise asserting the absolute "un-
lawfulness" of "stage entertainments"; Miss Boothby shared
his dislike of plays (except for *Irene!*). She had other dislikes:
fox hunting, Bath society, the "great," most novels (at least
she refused to read that improving work, *Sir Charles Grandison*), and London. Her taste in reading is sufficiently indicated

by the following passage from her first letter to Johnson: "How I should rejoice to see *your* pen *wholly* employed in the glorious Christian cause; inviting all into the ways of pleasantness; proving and displaying the only paths to peace! Whenever you have chosen this most interesting subject of Religion in your Ramblers, I have warmly wished you never to chuse any other" (pp. 37-38).

Now Johnson himself held no very high opinion of one or two of the items on her list of dislikes, yet he felt constrained to object. It seems clear that he believed certain of her condemnations too severe, too lacking in Christian charity. A case in point is what may be called the fox hunting controversy. In the letter in which she told Johnson that young William, the Fitzherbert son and heir, must be sent off to school, she asked Johnson for advice as to a suitable institution. Johnson recommended one; she asked for further details. In his reply Johnson evidently inquired what "indulgence" on Fitzherbert's part made it desirable that a boy so young should be sent from home. Miss Boothby, to her credit, was loath to criticize Fitzherbert, but in her reply she did reveal one reason for her decision. Young William's going from home, she writes, "and at a distance, I am sure you would see the necessity of, could I lay before you the reasons which daily urge me to feel it. Less evils must be submitted to, with the view of avoiding greater. I cannot help, with much pity, regarding a fox-hunter as an animal little superior to those he pursues, and dreading every path that seems to lead towards this miserable chace" (p. 66).

Perhaps Fitzherbert took the little boy with him on his hunts. At any rate, Johnson was not entirely satisfied with her answer. In later life he showed no objection to fox hunting; on the contrary, he boasted that he once "rode harder at a fox-chace than any body" (V, 253). On the present occasion, although he can hardly be said to have defended fox hunting, he remained disturbed, pointing out, if I interpret her reply correctly, that in his opinion the greater evil was sending a boy so young from home. Perhaps it is significant too that

58

for the first time he seems to have let slip that tact and defer-
ence with which he habitually addressed her. "You will never
provoke me to contradict you," she replies,

> unless you contradict me, without reasons and exempli-
> fication to support your opinion. 'Tis very true—all these
> things you have enumerated, are equally pitiable with a
> poor fox-hunter. 'Tis not in man to direct, either his own,
> or the way of others aright; nor do I ever look but to
> the supreme and all-wise Governor of the universe, either
> for direction, or with hope. I know you kindly mean to
> avert the pain of disappointment by discouraging expec-
> tation; but mine is never sanguine with regard to any
> thing here. . . . I like not the conclusion of your last
> letter; it is an ill compliment to call that mean, which the
> person you speak to most highly esteems and values.
> (pp. 70-71)

But what disturbed Johnson most was not her Puritanical
disapproval of what he regarded as relatively harmless amuse-
ments, or even, perhaps, the disdainful attitude she displayed
toward those who indulged in them (the "objects" she saw at
dinners, the fox hunting "animal"), but the fact that he sensed
in her religious principles a certain narrowness of outlook.
Did she believe salvation possible for many or few? For those
only who believed as she did, or for the many who differed
with her? Johnson, doubtful of his own worthiness, was always
anxious to spread the net of salvation as wide as possible. Was
her God really a God of Christian charity and benevolence?
Johnson, anxious to be reassured on this point, cited for her
consideration some Biblical texts which stressed the great
number of the "saved": the words of Jesus (Matt. 8: 11)—
"And I say unto you, That many shall come from east and
west, and shall sit down with Abraham, and Isaac, and Jacob,
in the kingdom of heaven"; and those of Daniel (7: 10, 14)—
"A fiery stream issued forth and came forth from before him:
thousand thousands ministered unto him; and ten thousand
times ten thousand stood before him: the judgment was set

and the books were opened . . . . And there was given him
dominion, and glory, and a kingdom, that all people, nations,
and languages, should serve him."

Her reply was, on the surface, reassuring enough:

> I utterly disclaim all faith that does not work by love,
> love that
>
> —Takes every creature in of every kind;
>
> and believe, from my soul, that in every sect and denomi-
> nation of Christians there are numbers, great numbers,
> who will sit down with Abraham, Isaac, and Jacob, and
> the promise, you quote, be gloriously fulfilled. I believe,
> and rejoice, in this assurance of happiness for ten thousand
> times ten thousand, thousand, &c. of every language and
> nation and people. I am convinced that many true Chris-
> tians differ; and if such do differ, it can be only in words,
> with regard to which great caution should be used.
> (p. 102)

Nevertheless, Miss Boothby knew that her own religious
outlook differed from Johnson's and she made a determined
effort to convert him to her own point of view. The first clear
foreshadowing of their subsequent disagreement comes fairly
early in the correspondence. Johnson had evidently inquired
as to her opinion of the place of morality or "good works" in
religion. Miss Boothby replies: "I will add a few more words,
though I am very busy; and a very few will fully shew my
thoughts on MORALITY. The Saviour of the world, Truth
itself, says, HE CAME NOT TO DESTROY THE LAW,
BUT TO FULFIL IT" (p. 47).

The place of morality or "good works" in God's plan for
salvation was one of the most important matters at issue between the Evangelicals and their opponents. Both parties
agreed that works without faith were vain; but the Evangelicals believed too many of the Anglican clergy and laity
preached up "reason" and "morality" at the expense of saving
faith, that they were really ignorant of what this doctrine

meant, and were inclined to believe that a life lived in accordance with generally accepted principles of morality was sufficient for salvation. Concerned to emphasize the utter inadequacy of good works without saving faith, the Evangelicals were sometimes accused of jettisoning morality altogether. A suspicion that Miss Boothby tended to underemphasize the importance of "works" may have crossed Johnson's mind, and though she reassures him on this point, the remainder of the correspondence makes it clear that for her, as for most Evangelicals, the question of works fades into the background by comparison with the overwhelming importance attached to the concept of saving faith. In the letter in which she defends herself against Johnson's charge of being too "abstracted" from common life, Miss Boothby goes on to state the fundamentals of her religious belief:

> We are all alike bad, my dear friend, depend upon it, till a change is wrought upon us, not by our own reasoning, but by the same Divine Power, who first created, and pronounced all he had made, *very good*. From this happy state we all plainly fell, and to it can we only be restored by the second Adam, who wrought out a full and complete redemption and restoration for us. Is this enthusiasm? Indeed it is truth: and, I trust, you will some time be sure it is so; and then, and not till then, will you be happy, as I ardently wish you. (pp. 95-96)

This sounds orthodox enough; why should she think Johnson hesitant to accept it as "truth"? Why should she fear he might suspect her of "enthusiasm," of a "vain belief of private revelation; a vain confidence of divine favour or communication"? Theological language is notoriously ambiguous. It is likely that neither Miss Boothby nor Johnson managed always to convey precisely what they intended; certainly Johnson, and perhaps Miss Boothby, suspected at times that their difference was "only in words" (p. 107). In explaining what I believe to be the central point at issue between them, I am clarifying what remains obscure in the correspondence itself. Evidence other than the correspondence is my warrant for this procedure; it shows, I think, that the difference between them was not semantic, but substantive.

In the first place, they held different views concerning the ability of the "natural" man to do good. Like many Evangelicals, Miss Boothby adheres to the Calvinistic doctrine of total depravity. Johnson never went so far. In conversation he could pass remarks on the depravity of human nature which would have satisfied the sternest Calvinist, but his considered opinion—expressed some five years before the date of this correspondence (in *Rambler* 70)—is that most men are neither greatly good nor greatly wicked. Johnson believes, as Miss Boothby does not, that most men, by an effort of will or "reasoning," may become, if not virtuous, at least more virtuous than they are. Made in the image of God, man is endowed at birth with a will potentially able to meet God halfway, as it were. Through his own efforts, with the help of God, he is able to work out his salvation. And so, for Johnson, the natural man is not utterly helpless, utterly depraved. One could almost say that Johnson had to believe this since in his own life he had not had any undoubted experience of "divine favour or communication"; that is, he had not experienced the kind of "conscious" conversion described in Chapter II, which is, for Miss Boothby, the indispensable means by which the believer acquires that saving faith without which all is lost. Not having experienced this "change wrought upon us" by the "Divine Power," Johnson, Miss Boothby believes, is still in an unregenerate state and will never be "happy" (acceptable to God) until he *has* experienced such a change. This point will be made clearer as we proceed; for the moment I would like to recall what was said of Evangelical attitudes toward the Christian evidences.

During the period of his correspondence with Miss Boothby, Johnson was working hard on the *Dictionary*. It was published in April 1755 and by early July Miss Boothby had her own copy "placed in full view" on a desk in her room. One wonders whether she noticed, among many citations of similar tendency, a quotation under the word "evidence" from Richard Bentley's *Confutation of Atheism* (1692). Bentley points out that "there are books extant, which they [atheists] must allow of as proper *evidence;* even the mighty volumes of visible nature, and the everlasting tables of right reason." At any rate, it is the evidences which are at issue in Miss Boothby's next letter to Johnson. The lady writes:

> I am desirous that, in the great and one thing necessary, you should think as I do; and I am persuaded you some time will. I will not enter into a controversy with you. I am sure I can never this way convince you in any point wherein we differ; nor can any mortal convince me, by human arguments, that there is not a divine evidence for divine truths. Such the Apostle plainly defines Faith to be, when he tells us, it is *'the substance of things hoped for, the evidence of things not seen.'* Human testimony can go no farther than things seen, and visible to the senses. Divine and spiritual things are far above—and what says St. Paul?—*'For what man knoweth the things of a man, save the spirit of man which is in him? Even so the things of God knoweth no man, but the spirit of God?'* Do, read the whole chapter [I Cor. 2] and, if you please, Mr. Romaine's Sermon, or Discourse, lately published [1755], *on the benefit, which the Holy Spirit of God is of to man in his journey through life.* (pp. 100-102)

No man can know the things of God, but *by* the active agency of the spirit of God working within him. In other words, the reason of the natural man, reason uninspired by "the spirit of God," is of no value in establishing the truths of religion. For Miss Boothby the mere attempt to establish religious truth in this way is vain since, as the essence of religion is inward and spiritual, and therefore far above "things seen, and visible to the senses," so a method of "proof" which derives its support from these things can never bring saving conviction because it can never touch the core of religion at all. That this is an accurate statement of Hill Boothby's interpretation of the Pauline text is clear, I think, from the tract by the well-known Evangelical clergyman William Romaine which she recommends to Johnson. When Romaine wrote this tract he had already "passed entirely to the side of Whitefield . . . and from that time to the end of his life he remained the ablest exponent among the evangelicals of the highest Calvinistic doctrine, holding Wesley's views, especially in the matter of free will and perfection, as a subtle reproduction of the Romish theory of justification by works" (*DNB*). Since Romaine's tract leans heavily upon I Corinthians 2, and is in large part simply Romaine's explication of that chapter, we may be confident that Hill Boothby fully agrees with Romaine's interpretation. She wants Johnson to study this chapter in the light of Romaine's commentary, trusting that he will then come to a true understanding of what is meant by saving faith, "the great and one thing necessary."

And what does saving faith mean for Romaine? First of all, it is an inward experience; it needs no support from "human testimony":

> And whoever has received these ordinary operations of the Holy Spirit, has in his own heart clear and full testimony of the Godhead, and almighty power of the blessed Spirit. He wants no outward miracles. This great inward work is to him complete evidence; and he is able to rest his salvation with as full trust and confidence upon it, as if he had seen the apostles exert their miraculous gifts and graces.[8]

Second, "the mighty volumes of visible nature, and the everlasting tables of right reason" are of no use whatever in leading mankind to a saving faith in the truths of Christianity:

> The natural understanding in its highest refinement cannot discover them [the things of God]; 'for the natural man receiveth not the things of the Spirit of God, for they are foolishness unto him, neither can he know them, because they are spiritually discerned.' (I Cor. 2:14) The natural man cannot receive spiritual things. God must reveal them unto him by his Spirit before he can have the least discernment of them, even what is revealed concerning them in scripture cannot be discerned, until the Holy Spirit open the eyes to behold it. (p. 279)

Third, this enlightenment, or "conversion," as we may properly call it, takes place in a moment of time, and the person so converted is fully conscious of the experience he has undergone: "Do you remember when the Holy Spirit opened your eyes, and brought you out of darkness into his marvellous light?" (p. 286). Fourth, all men can do to acquire this experience is earnestly and prayerfully to seek the assistance of the Holy Spirit, but this is the Holy Spirit's own work:

> We must plead and intreat, and importune you to seek his assistance, but the success must come from him. The word itself is but a dead letter, unless he animate it; and therefore the preaching of it can have no power, unless he accompany it. We may plant and water, but he must give the increase. (pp. 288-89)

Finally, without such a conversion, all is lost:

> If you call yourselves Christians, and yet know nothing of those great changes, which the holy Spirit must work in your hearts before you are Christians indeed, O consider in what a dangerous state you live. If God be true, your souls are in darkness, your hearts in sin, and all your faculties under the power of Satan, and until you be enlightened and converted, have a new heart and a new nature, you are children of wrath, and if you die in this state, you are lost and ruined to all eternity. If ever you see the face of God with joy, you must be renewed in the spirit of your mind. You must be made just and holy. All this must be done. You must experience it, and you will know it as certainly as you know any truth, when the holy Spirit bears testimony with your spirits, that you are the children of God.
>
> But you have been told that this doctrine is enthusiasm .... (p. 286)

We don't know whether Johnson read Romaine's tract, but two months later we find Miss Boothby expressing her regret "that the text in Corinthians does not prove to you what I would have it," and praying "that it may prove it" (p. 124). Johnson's reaction was disappointing, but Miss Boothby did not abandon her efforts to convert him to her views concerning "the great and one thing necessary." In her next letter she writes: "Have you read Mr. Law? not cursorily, but with attention? I wish you would consider him; *'His appeal to all that doubt*, &c.' I think the most clear of all his later writings; and, in recommending it to you, I shall say no more or less than what you will see he says in his *Advertisement to the Reader*" (p. 127).[8a]

Johnson had of course read Law's *Serious Call* "with attention"; but we know that he disapproved of Law's later writings, influenced as these were by what Johnson called "the reveries of Jacob Behmen" (II, 122). Perhaps he first became acquainted with these at Miss Boothby's urging. It is clear that she persuaded him to read at least one of them, and to read it "with attention." In her last surviving letter, dated in Johnson's hand "December 1755," she remarks that she has sent him "a little book." "I have read your book," replies Johnson in his letter of December 31, 1755. Not only has he read it but he has commented upon it, and fearful that these comments might be read by eyes other than hers asks that she return the book: "I beg you to return the book when you have looked into it. I should not have written what is in the margin, had I not had it from you, or had I not intended to show it you" (Letter 79). In his last letter to her, written eight days before her death, he writes: "I have returned your *Law* which however I earnestly entreat you to give me" (Letter 84). It seems clear that Miss Boothby's "little book" and Johnson's "Law" are one and the same. Aside from the fact that Johnson wants both the "little book" and the "Law" returned to him, the dates for this part of the correspondence, covering hardly more than a month, would not seem to allow for the exchange in this manner of two different books. The book in question may well have been Law's *An Appeal to all that doubt, or disbelieve the truths of the Gospel, whether they be Deists, Arians, Socinians, or* Nominal *Christians* (1740). (Did Miss Boothby believe Johnson a "nominal"

Christian?). Miss Boothby is quite right in thinking this the clearest of Law's later writings; if she knew Johnson at all well, she would have hesitated to send him one of Law's more intensely mystical tracts.

But her recommendation of the *Appeal* is of great interest, whether it is this or another of Law's tracts that Johnson actually commented upon, since the *Appeal* indicates clearly what Miss Boothby valued in the later Law. The *Appeal* had the merit, from her point of view, of setting forth with much greater eloquence and elaboration of detail, the same view of saving faith that Romaine had presented in his tract on the Holy Spirit. Taking the whole universe for his province, Law launches an elaborate investigation in which he attempts to prove that God "created man in the image of His Holy Trinity."[9] But Law's theology is in essence simply an elaborate "proof upon proof" of the same view of saving faith that Romaine held, and this is no doubt why Miss Boothby recommended the book to Johnson. If Corinthians or Romaine had not convinced him of "the great and one thing necessary," perhaps the eloquent Law would. And Law is quite clear about the "great and one thing necessary":

> Now if this Light and Spirit of Heaven is *generated* in your Soul as it is generated in Heaven, if it arises up in your Nature *within* you, as it does in eternal Nature *without* you, (which is the Christian new Birth, or Regeneration) then you are become capable of the Kingdom of Heaven, and nothing can keep you out of it; but if you die without this Birth of the Eternal Light and Spirit of God, then your Soul stands in the *same Distance* from, and *Contrariety* to the Kingdom of Heaven as Hell does: If you die in this unregenerate State, it signifies nothing *how* you have lived, or *what* Religion you have owned, all is left undone that was to have saved you: It matters not what *Form* of Life you have appeared in, what a Number of decent, engaging or glorious Exploits you have done either as a *Scholar*, a *Statesman*, or a *Philosopher;* if they have proceeded only from the Light and Spirit of

this World, they must die with it, and leave your Soul in that Eternal Darkness, which it must have, so long as the Light and Spirit of Eternity is not generated in it.[10]

There is nothing here which Romaine, or most Evangelicals, could not have wholeheartedly endorsed.

What was Johnson's reaction to Miss Boothby's book? The letter of December 31, in which he gives it, is the last letter in which he discusses religion with her. "My Sweet Angel," he writes,

> I have read your book, I am afraid you will think without any great improvement, whether you can read my notes I know not. You ought not to be offended, I am perhaps as sincere as the writer. In all things that terminate here I shall be much guided by your influence, and should take or leave by your direction, but I cannot receive my religion from any human hand. I desire however to be instructed and am far from thinking myself perfect . . . .
>
> It affords me a new conviction that in these books there is little new, except new forms of expression, which may be sometimes taken even by the writer, for new doctrines. (Letter 79)

"I cannot receive my religion from any human hand." Baretti comments: "He would certainly have taken it from her without ever suspecting he did."[11] It is idle to speculate on what would have happened if Miss Boothby had lived. But it is worth noting that there is nothing in the correspondence to show that Johnson was beginning to accommodate his position to hers; on the contrary, at the beginning of the correspondence Johnson, then uncertain of her religious position, is tentative and questioning. As he learns more about her views, he becomes more assertive, until finally he is constrained, however deferentially and politely, to reject these views. To be sure, he is still willing "to be instructed" but one wonders what further artillery she could have brought to bear. If Johnson could not accept her reading of 1 Corinthians 2 as we have seen it expounded by Romaine, he had failed to accept the essence of her Evangelical faith. The eloquent Law met with no more acceptance; what other "human hand" might have overcome his doubts?

Johnson questions whether there are any new doctrines in Miss Boothby's book, and here he is supported by modern students who agree that the differences between the Evangelicals and their opponents involve matters of emphasis, not matters of doctrine. The Evangelicals "revived" the doctrine of saving faith from, as they saw it, the neglect into which it had fallen. Associating this doctrine with a particular sort of conversion experience (not itself a matter of doctrine at all), they tended to stress the depravity of fallen man beyond what many Anglicans thought reasonable, needful, or Scriptural. Here the Evangelicals could appeal to the Thirty-nine Articles just as their opponents could appeal to them, with perhaps equal reason, to justify a less extreme view.

But differences of emphasis can be vastly important as the history of the Evangelical revival amply demonstrates, and Johnson, I believe, saw at the time that the difference between his own religious outlook and that of Miss Boothby was considerable and important. Because he loved and admired Miss Boothby, he was polite, deferential, and perhaps did not always say exactly what he thought. But that remark "I cannot receive my religion from any human hand" is rather definite, and after Miss Boothby's death, Johnson did not hesitate to give his frank opinion of her religious outlook. Although praising her purity of mind and her graces of manner, he told Mrs. Thrale that "she pushed her piety to bigotry, her devotion to enthusiasm."[12] I believe Johnson was choosing his words with care and this time meant exactly what he said. "Bigotry" Johnson defines as "blind zeal; prejudice; unreasonable warmth in favour of party or opinions." With reference to Miss Boothby it points to her unwavering conviction that there is only one way to salvation and that she and those of like mind have the key. If there is one thing the *Rambler* essays demonstrate over and over again, it is Johnson's belief in the enormous capacity for self-delusion, the great difficulty of seeing a thing as it is and not as we wish it to be. Johnson simply could not believe that "divine evidence for divine truths" was *ordinarily* granted to even the most devout Christians. It was more likely that the believer had deceived himself than that he had been the recipient of such an extraordinary experience. "Favourable impressions," he remarked in 1781,

> as to the state of our souls, may be deceitful and dangerous. In general no man can be sure of his acceptance with GOD; some, indeed, may have had it revealed to them. St. Paul, who wrought miracles, may have had a miracle wrought on himself, and may have obtained supernatural assurance of pardon, and mercy, and beatitude; yet St. Paul, though he expresses strong hope, also expresses fear, lest having preached to others, he himself should be a cast-away. (IV, 123)

And in the last year of his life, talking of the fear of death, he said that "some people are not afraid, because they look upon salvation as the effect of an absolute decree, and think they feel in themselves the marks of sanctification. Others, and those the most rational in my opinion, look upon salvation as conditional; and as they never can be sure that they have complied with the conditions, they are afraid" (IV, 278). Johnson could have agreed with Law in the *Appeal* that conversion means a man has become "capable of the Kingdom of Heaven"; he would *never* have added, as Law does, that once a man has experienced this conversion nothing can keep him *out* of that kingdom.

I believe, then, that we must associate the religious outlook of the mature Johnson, not with the Evangelical Anglicanism of men like Hervey, Berridge, Grimshaw, Romaine, or Cowper, but with that tradition of "rational" Anglicanism which, descending from Hooker, includes such men as South, Clarke, Tillotson, and Butler.[13] I will attempt in Part II to define more precisely Johnson's relationship to this tradition.

Part II

V

Johnson and the Christian Evidences

WE HAVE SEEN that for Evangelicals like Miss Boothby and William Romaine, the "inward work" of the Holy Spirit brought with it full conviction of the truths of revelation; the Evangelicals needed no outward proofs. On the other hand, Johnson, it has been said, "accepted the Bible as revelation, but only because he had, or thought he had, good rational reasons for believing that it *was* revelation. In other words, his arguments in favor of the Christian religion were founded almost exclusively upon an acceptance of those 'Christian evidences' which seemed so much more solid than they have seemed, even to most churchmen, in any century since his own."[1]

This is true, but somewhat misleading. Certainly it is impossible to imagine Johnson being attracted to an orthodoxy which deliberately proclaimed its irrationality. The Anglican tradition in which he had been raised assumed, as a matter of course, that reason and revelation were not imcompatible. Revelation is above reason, not contrary to it. It follows that human reason can make certain limited discoveries concerning the "things of God." At the same time, since religion is a way of looking at things involving the whole man, it is hard to believe that anyone was ever converted to Christianity, or to any religion, through reasoning alone. As Professor Matson puts it, "no one ever said to himself: 'I wonder whether there is a God? I hear Smith's book is the latest thing on the subject.

They say he sets out the evidence most fairly, and evaluates the inferences quite dispassionately and judiciously. I had better read him before making up my mind.' "[2] Certainly, it was not an argument on the validity of the Christian evidences which first led Johnson to think earnestly of religion. This is only to say that Johnson's adherence to orthodoxy is not, in the first instance, a matter of his belief in the "reasonableness" of Christianity. He knew very well, as we shall see, that faith is one thing, that arguments in support of it are another, and that, in the nature of the case, these arguments are not "irresistible"—they cannot compel belief. But Johnson, like most Anglicans of his day, "was anxious that his beliefs should appear reasonable to others,"[3] and he lived at a time when the most formidable threat to orthodoxy expressed itself in deistic and sceptical attacks on revelation as irrational, hence unworthy of belief by men of education and intelligence.

It will be appropriate to begin with Johnson's attitude toward the evidences as a whole. How strong are they? Johnson is quite clear on this point. When Boswell once asked him if any man has "the same conviction of the truth of Religion that he has in the common affairs of life," Johnson replied simply, "No, Sir."[4] For Johnson this follows from the nature of religion itself. In his review of Soame Jenyns' *Free Enquiry into the Nature and Origin of Evil,* Johnson remarks that Jenyns says nothing of religion "but what he has learned, or might have learned, from the divines; that it is not universal, because it must be received upon conviction, and successively received by those whom conviction reached; that its evidences and sanctions are not irresistible, because it was intended to induce, not to compel; that it is obscure, because we want faculties to comprehend it."[5]

Johnson agrees with the divines. Were the evidences irresistible, there would be no room for faith. Johnson's definitions of the term "faith" in the *Dictionary* indicate his awareness of the theological distinction between *fides,* or belief, and *fiducia,* or trust. One has faith (*fides*) that God exists and that certain propositions about him are true. "Here 'faith' is used cognitively, referring to a state, act, or procedure which may be compared with standard instances of knowing and believing." *Fiducia,* on the other hand, "is a religious trust which may be compared with trust or confidence in another human person."[6] Defining faith as *fides* or "belief of the revealed truths of religion," Johnson has in mind the second use when under this definition he quotes Hooker: "The name of *faith* being properly and strictly taken, it must needs have reference unto some uttered word, as the object of belief." One's trust or confidence in the gospel promises (the "uttered word") is based upon a faith in Christ comparable to the trust or confidence one places in a "human person." Because one believes that Christ is what he proclaims himself to be, one accepts many things in the New Testament which seem obscure, just as one accepts the word of a trusted friend although what he says may seem illogical or unreasonable. Another citation under Johnson's definition of faith are the following lines from Matthew Prior's "Charity: A Paraphrase on the Thirteenth Chapter of the First Epistle to the Corinthians," a poem Johnson pronounced "eminently beautiful":[7]

> Then *faith* shall fail, and holy hope shall die;
> One lost in certainty, and one in joy.

At the Last Day faith shall be transformed into certainty, but until then faith for Johnson is belief based upon credible but not demonstrative evidence.

On one occasion, at least, Johnson used the argument of Bishop Butler in his *Analogy of Religion* that "*he who believes the Scripture to have proceeded from him who is the Author of Nature, may well expect to find the same sort of difficulties in it as are found in the constitution of Nature.*"[8] Faced with the religious "uneasiness" of the blind poet Thomas Blacklock, Johnson "encouraged the blind Bard to apply to higher speculations what we all willingly submit to in common life: in short, he gave him more familiarly the able and fair reasoning of Butler's *Analogy.*" "Why, sir," said Johnson, "the greatest concern we have in *this* world [my italics], the choice of our profession, must be determined without demonstrative reasoning. Human life is not yet so well known, as that we can have it. And take the case of a man who is ill. I call two physicians: they differ in opinion. I am not to lie down, and die between them: I must do something"(V, 47).

"I must do something." Johnson was well aware of what has now become a commonplace: the idea of religious commitment as involving risk. In Johnson's day the locus classicus for this idea was Pascal's *Pensées*, a book Johnson knew well. No one knows what Johnson thought of Pascal's famous "wager"; we do know that he approved the *Pensées* as a "pious" book.[9] He knew as well as Pascal that religious commitment involves risk, but he believed the Christian evidences solid enough to justify a reasonable man in taking that risk.

What sort of proofs, then, did he find most satisfying? Johnson once recommended Hugo Grotius' *De Veritate Religionis*, John Pearson's *An Exposition of the Creed*, and Samuel Clarke's *A Demonstration of the Being and Attributes of God* "to every man whose faith is yet unsettled" (I, 398). All three books, as S. G. Brown says, "contain what is essentially the same argument: metaphysical demonstration of a First Cause in the manner of Aristotle, and identification of the First Cause with the Christian God."[10] We may say with some confidence that the first part of this argument seems never to have posed much of a problem for Johnson. He tells us elsewhere that we have "demonstration for a First Cause" (III, 316) and he defines "demonstration" as "the highest degree of deducible or argumental evidence; the strongest degree of proof; such proof as not only evinces the position proved to be true, but shows the contrary position to be absurd and impossible." "Turn matter on all sides," he once wrote, "make it eternal, or of late production, finite or infinite, there can be no regular system produced, but by a voluntary and meaning agent."[11] Johnson, like the physico-theologians, assumes that the system *is* "regular"; hence the product of an intelligent Maker. For Johnson, as for most of his contemporaries, it was more difficult to conceive of a universe without a Maker than with one. The major alternative to theism known to them—the atomistic theory of the ancients—was rarely a difficulty since the idea of a universe of order arising out of chaos without the intervention of intelligence put a more serious strain upon credibility than the contrary supposition. During the seventeenth century it was easier to take atomism seriously but, after Newton, orthodox Christians could invoke the name of the greatest scientist of the western world in behalf of the regularity of nature's processes. And the greater the regularity, the greater the necessity for an Intelligent Regulator. Thus, in the *Dictionary* under "atheist" Johnson quotes Creech:

> Atheist, use thine eyes,
> And, having viewed the order of the skies,
> Think, if thou canst, that matter, blindly hurl'd
> Without a guide, should frame this wondrous world.

To be sure, atheists existed; even the demonstration of a First Cause was not "irresistible" to all men. But a simple theism, positing no more than a First Cause endowed with intelligence and power was, I think, a belief that Johnson accepted easily enough. Nor does he seem to have believed atheism widespread in his own day. When he accuses Hume or Gibbon of "infidelity" he is not accusing them of atheism. In the *Dictionary* the atheist is "one that denies the existence of God"; the infidel, on the other hand, is "an unbeliever; a miscreant; a pagan; one who rejects Christianity," and infidelity is "want of faith" and "disbelief of Christianity." The nearest Johnson seems to have come in accusing any one of his contemporaries of atheism is his remark that Hume "if he is anything . . . is a Hobbist," Hobbism being generally considered the equivalent of atheism—but on another occasion he implies that he thought Hume a deist.[12] I believe Johnson would have agreed with Bishop Butler that the existence of

> an intelligent Author of Nature, and *natural* Governor of the world . . . has been often proved with accumulated evidence; from this argument of analogy and final causes, from abstract reasoning, from the most ancient tradition and testimony, and from the general consent of mankind. Nor does it appear, so far as I can find, to be denied by the

generality of those who profess themselves dissatisfied with the evidence of religion [i.e., orthodox Christianity].[13]

The real difficulty for Johnson lay in the identification of this First Cause with the God of the Bible. A First Cause *might* be morally neutral; Christians had to show that this First Cause possessed the moral attributes of the Biblical God. They had then to show that the central doctrines of Christian faith were precisely those which such a God might be expected to reveal to men at a particular moment in time, to a particular small section of humanity, and in a manner contravening all known laws of nature. In the following passage, it seems to me that Johnson is using the forcible word "demonstration" in connection at most with only two of the divine attributes—those of intelligence and power. The one crucial to his argument—goodness—he appears to regard as less clearly self-evident:

> Sir, you cannot answer all objections. You have demonstration for a First Cause: you see he must be good as well as powerful, because there is nothing to make him otherwise, and goodness of itself is preferable. Yet you have against this, what is very certain, the unhappiness of human life. This, however, gives us reason to hope for a future state of compensation, that there may be a perfect system. But of what we were not sure, til we had a positive revelation. (III, 316-17)

It is clear that Johnson approved the traditional arguments for theism to which Butler refers, and that he believed men like Grotius, Pearson, Clarke, and, we may add, physico-theologians like Ray, Blackmore, Burnet, Derham, and Bentley,[14] had presented arguments which were valid so far as they went.

Two types of proof are conspicuous in these writers. There is first the high priori road best represented by Clarke's *Demonstration of the Being and Attributes of God* (1704-5). Clarke, a mathematical rationalist, considering pure reason sufficient to establish the existence of a First Cause together with most, at least, of the necessary moral attributes, relegates arguments drawn from sense experience to a secondary position. The physico-theologians, on the other hand, argue a posteriori from the existence of design and purposeful adaptation in the natural world to the existence of an intelligent Designer. It should be said at once that the latter method was by far the most popular in the eighteenth century. The argument from (or to) Design is very ancient, but it received, most people thought, additional confirmation from the scientific achievements of the period. Thus, the argument from Design, reinforced by the findings of seventeenth- and eighteenth-century science, came to be "regarded by the Age of Reason as one of its great triumphs."[15] A true scientist, a Ray or a Newton, could give the argument the solid weight that attaches to empirical fact, but it required no training in philosophy and little knowledge of science to appreciate the force of the argument. Clarke himself recognized this, and at the end of his *Demonstration*, admitting that not all men were philosophers enough to understand his a priori demonstration, goes on to insist that such men were "utterly without Excuse" if they refused to accept theism. They had only to look about them since

> the Notices that God has been pleased to give us of himself, are so many and so obvious; in the Constitution, Order, Beauty, and Harmony of the several Parts of the World; in the Frame and Structure of our own Bodies, and the wonderful Powers and Faculties of our Souls; in the unavoidable Apprehensions of our own Minds, and the common Consent of all other Men; in every thing within us, and every thing without us: that no Man of the meanest Capacity and greatest Disadvantages whatsoever, with the slightest and most superficial Observation of the Works of God, and the lowest and most obvious attendance to the Reason of Things, can be ignorant of *Him*.[16]

All eighteenth-century arguments in favor of orthodoxy may be divided into two great classes with reference to their bearing upon natural or revealed religion. The arguments we have been considering here bear upon the former. They do not pretend to give us the God of the Bible; rather they intend to show that the God men may discover by the use of reason and observation bears a remarkable resemblance to the God of revelation. But the argument is not complete until revelation itself has been shown to be solidly grounded, and fully "consonant," as Clarke puts it, "to the Dictates of sound Reason, or the unprejudiced Light of Nature."[17]

Johnson's own method of "establishing" revelation is the common-sense one of attempting to show that the events narrated in the Bible—at least those important to Christians—are solidly grounded in fact. It is clear that *all* arguments in favor of theism, or "natural religion," as the eighteenth century called it, seemed to Johnson less important than those which tended to establish revelation itself as solidly grounded in the facts of history. The reason is obvious enough. As an eminent Protestant theologian of our own day puts it, "theism is very different from belief in God. Necessary Being—the *ens necessarium* of scholastic philosophy—is not the God and Father of our Lord Jesus Christ."[18] Even if Clarke, or another, had convinced Johnson that this Necessary Being had all the *moral* attributes of the Christian God—that he was good as well as great—the question would still remain: why this *particular* method of dealing with mankind rather than another? Why the Incarnation, the Atonement, the Resurrection? One should never forget Johnson's sense of the utter gratuitousness of existence. As he told Boswell (III, 342), "There are innumerable questions to which the inquisitive mind can in this state receive no answer: Why do you and I exist? Why was this world created? Since it was to be created, why was it not created sooner?" Given the fact of creation, a wise and benevolent God might conceivably have chosen some other method of dealing with the creatures he had made. Thus Johnson was not satisfied with evidence pointing up similarities between the God of Nature and the God of the Bible. What he wanted was evidence to show that, of all possible modes of the God-man relationship, the Christian revelation was *in fact* the one chosen by God. The fullest and clearest instance of

Johnson's appeal to the facts of history is doubly significant because he made it at a time when he knew he was dying. William Windham asked Johnson's opinion of "natural and revealed religion." Bypassing the traditional theistic proofs, Johnson chose to discuss revealed religion only:

> For revealed religion [Johnson said], there was such historical evidence, as, upon any subject not religious, would have left no doubt. Had the facts recorded in the New Testament been mere civil occurrences, no one would have called in question the testimony by which they are established; but the importance annexed to them, amounting to nothing less than the salvation of mankind, *raised a cloud* in our minds, and created doubts unknown upon any other subject. Of proofs to be derived from history, one of the most cogent, he seemed to think, was the opinion so well authenticated, and so long entertained, of a Deliverer that was to appear about that time. . . . For the immediate life and miracles of Christ, such attestation as that of the apostles, who all, except St. John, confirmed their testimony with their blood; such belief as their witness procured from a people best furnished with the means of judging, and least disposed to judge favourably; such an extension afterwards of that belief over all the nations of the earth, though originating from a nation of all others most despised, would leave no doubt that the things witnessed were true, and were of a nature more than human. With respect to evidence, Dr. Johnson observed that we had not such evidence that Caesar died in the Capitol, as that Christ died in the manner related. (*JM*, II, 384)

Johnson reinforces this type of reasoning with another. Talking of those who denied the truth of Christianity, he said,

> It is always easy to be on the negative side. If a man were now to deny that there is salt upon the table, you could not reduce him to an absurdity. Come, let us try this a

little further. I deny that Canada is taken, and I can support my denial by pretty good arguments. The French are a much more numerous people than we; and it is not likely that they would allow us to take it. 'But the ministry have assured us, in all the formality of the Gazette, that it is taken.'—Very true. But the ministry have put us to an enormous expence by the war in America, and it is their interest to persuade us that we have got something for our money.—'But the fact is confirmed by thousands of men who were at the taking of it.'—Ay, but these men have still more interest in deceiving us. They don't want that you should think the French have beat them, but that they have beat the French. Now suppose you should go over and find that it is really taken, that would only satisfy yourself; for when you come home we will not believe you. We will say, you have been bribed.—Yet, Sir, notwithstanding all these plausible objections, we have no doubt that Canada is really ours. Such is the weight of common testimony. How much stronger are the evidences of the Christian religion? (I, 428)

This argument is an interesting anticipation of a once famous essay (still occasionally reprinted) by Richard Whately entitled "Historic Doubts Relative to Napoleon Buonaparte" (1819).[19] Arguing against Hume's essay on miracles, Whately attempts to show that *all* testimony is vulnerable in just the ways outlined by Johnson—yet we accept the testimony. It is therefore no more unreasonable to accept the testimony in favor of revelation than it is to accept that in favor of any well-attested historical fact.

The two passages I have quoted above, presenting what has been aptly called "the argument from testimony and comparative credibility,"[20] sum up what Johnson thought to be the most convincing "proofs" of the Christian revelation. It may be said—and the popularity of Whately's essay may be some evidence of this—that they probably compose the strongest defense that could have been given at the time (I am, of course, ignoring evidence derived from one's personal experience of the Christian life, as well as arguments which attempt to prove the existence of God from the nature of man).[20a] Before the inauguration of the "higher criticism" of the Bible, before the advent of studies in comparative religion and in the psychology and sociology of religion, it was still possible to assume with Johnson that the Bible in most of its aspects is straightforward history, similar in this respect to secular history, and that the testimony in favor of the one is to be weighed and evaluated in precisely the same manner as that in favor of the other. The disciplines, historical, philological, archaeological, and so on, which have since shown considerable parts of the Bible to be myth, legend, or folklore, were as yet in a rudimentary state of development. But if it was hardly possible as yet to mount a wholly convincing attack upon the Biblical text itself, there was another way of undermining the kind of arguments Johnson uses in support of revelation.

Already in Johnson's lifetime the Christian evidences had undergone the incisive criticism of his great contemporary, David Hume. That Johnson recognized Hume as the most dangerous contemporary opponent of orthodoxy seems clear enough.[21] How well Johnson understood the particular character and implications of Hume's critique of religion is another matter.

In 1748 Hume had published his *Philosophical Essays concerning Human Understanding*. His notorious essay "Of Miracles" appeared there as Section X, where it was followed by Section XI, "Of the Practical Consequences of Natural Religion" (later called "Of a Particular Providence and of a Future State"). Deliberately and ironically provocative beyond any other of Hume's writings on religion, "Of Miracles" soon caught the attention of the public and has remained ever since one of Hume's best known works. Attacking miracles, Hume's essay is a direct attack upon revelation since the New Testament miracles were considered evidence of Christ's divinity.

Boswell was fascinated by Hume's argument, and Boswell, querying Johnson, has left on record a few Johnsonian remarks in reply to Hume.[22] Johnson simply reiterates his belief that miracles are possible, and then proceeds to defend the New

Testament miracles by arguments we have seen him use in defense of revelation generally. But I waive consideration of Johnson's remarks because I believe Hume's miracles essay more vulnerable to criticism than its sequel, Section XI. Some students of Hume think Sections X and XI should be read together as forming a single argument.[23] If Hume's eighteenth-century critics failed to do this, Hume himself is partly to blame. When he announced at the beginning of his essay that he had discovered a "decisive" argument against miracles, he encouraged his critics to concentrate their fire upon Section X as a self-contained unit.

This is what Johnson's Oxford friend William Adams does in his *Essay on Mr. Hume's Essay on Miracles* (1751), and Johnson thought Adams had "confuted" Hume.[24] Adams, at least, points to weaknesses which are really present in Hume's essay. Agreeing with Hume that the credibility of any fact depends upon its analogy to the known course of nature, Adams remarks that "the powers of nature are so imperfectly known to us, that in most cases we argue with great uncertainty from this principle,"[25] and hence must often rely upon testimony for the truth of past events. This is a valid criticism, for, as a modern critic says, Hume, defining a miracle as a "violation" of a law of nature, "in trying to show that a miracle must always be less credible than the corresponding natural law contrasts the testimony in support of a miracle with the observed regularities in which the law consists," as though our knowledge of these "observed regularities" were exhaustive.[26] But against this Adams can cite new scientific discoveries: who in the past could have supposed "that an animal might be propagated by cutting it in pieces"? Hume "tells us that we must judge of testimony by experience," but there is considerable truth in Adams' reply that "it is more certain that we must judge of the experience of men by their testimony."[27] I would argue, not that Adams has "confuted" Hume, but that he has given some reason to believe that the argument of Section X is not, as Hume thought, "decisive" in demonstrating the a priori impossibility of miracles.

I doubt, then, that Hume's argument really disturbed Johnson, whatever Boswell's reaction to it. It is worth noting that Johnson discusses "Hume on Miracles" with temperateness, whereas on the occasion of his most violent outburst against Hume (V, 29-30) Johnson had in mind James Beattie's attack on Hume's philosophy *as a whole* in Beattie's *Essay on Truth* (1770), and Beattie deliberately omits detailed discussion of the miracles essay since he believes Hume has been "confuted with great elegance and precision, and with invincible force of argument"[28] by George Campbell in the latter's *Dissertation on Miracles* (1762), the best and most elaborate contemporary reply to Hume's essay.

But whether one thinks Hume's essay vulnerable to criticism or not, one can make a good case for the view expressed many years ago by W. R. Sorley that the controversy over Hume's essay was, and is, "a side issue."[29] According to this view—which I adopt here—the real strength of Hume's polemic against orthodoxy is to be found in his attack upon the Design and First Cause arguments, and this attack, presented in Section XI and in the *Dialogues concerning Natural Religion*, constitutes, I would argue, a telling critique upon virtually the whole of natural religion as it was understood in the eighteenth century.

Hume, in Section XI, undermining the usual theistic proofs, also rules out any sort of supernaturalism. If one accepts Hume's reasoning as valid, the "God" that remains is, as Kemp Smith has said, not the sort of deity to whom "the Scriptural or other miracles can fittingly be ascribed."[30] Hume need not have discussed miracles at all. If his reasoning in Section XI and in the *Dialogues* is accepted, the term "miracle" can mean no more than an extraordinary but entirely "natural" event. One contemporary critic, at least, seems to have understood this. In 1749 William Warburton, in a letter to a friend, remarked that Hume in his *Philosophical Essays* argues in one part "against the being of a God, [surely a reference to Section XI] and in another, (very needlessly you will say,) against the possibility of miracles."[31] If Hume is right, human reason and observation can make no valid inferences concerning either the existence or the nature of God. Belief in revelation, then, must be wholly a matter of faith; it can receive no support from any other source.

If Hume's examination of the Design and First Cause arguments constitutes his most telling critique of orthodoxy, we naturally want to know Johnson's reaction. But all we know is that Johnson did read Beattie's *Essay on Truth* and that Johnson, like many others, thought Beattie had "confuted" Hume (V, 274).

Beattie, at least, begins in the right way. He attempts to undermine the basic principles of Hume's philosophy as expounded, especially, in the *Treatise of Human Nature*. In particular, he tries to show that Hume's theory of causation is nonsense. And in the process he comes to grips with Hume's critique of the Design and First Cause arguments. The fifth section of Beattie's second chapter, entitled "Of Reasoning from the Effect to the Cause," is a direct attack upon Section XI. But Beattie, like so many others, failed to understand Hume. One result of this general misunderstanding is, as Kant said, that Hume's opponents "were ever assuming as conceded what he doubted, and demonstrating with eagerness and often with arrogance what he never thought of disputing."[32] Beattie's chapter against Section XI provides a good example of this. Beattie, combining certain of Hume's phrases with others of his own composition, sums up Hume's "very strange argument . . . against the belief of a Deity" as follows:

> The universe . . . is an object quite singular and unparalleled; no other object that has fallen under our observation bears any similarity to it; neither it nor its cause can be comprehended under any known species; and therefore concerning the cause of the universe we can form no rational conclusion at all.[33]

This is an accurate summary of Hume's argument if, instead of Beattie's final clause, we substitute the words "we can form no rational conclusion for assigning to this cause the attributes of the Christian God."

But Beattie, giving a reasonable approximation of Hume's

argument, then proceeds to ignore or misrepresent it. Reading Beattie, one would think Hume had argued for an "uncaused" universe, and while it is true that in the *Dialogues* (which Beattie could not have seen) Hume "raises the question whether the very conception of First Cause is not logically and empirically unjustifiable,"[34] he does *not* do this in Section XI. On the contrary, he argues that even if the validity of the argument from Design is granted, "namely, that there exists an Author of nature," this is a useless conclusion for religion since we may never legitimately "attribute to the cause any property over and above those it must have in order to produce the effect." Therefore, "we are not justified in attributing to the Author of Nature omnipotence, wisdom or goodness"—much less the gift of eternal life—"for these properties are not required to account for the natural phenomena as we have them."[35]

Hume does not argue, as Beattie strongly implies, that there is *no* "rational" cause of the universe; he merely maintains that we can never know anything certain *about* this cause, including the question of its supposed "rationality." This being the case, it is somewhat beside the point for Beattie to spend by far the greater part of his chapter establishing the solidity of the maxim that "whatever beginneth to exist, proceedeth from some cause," as though Hume had denied this. For even though Beattie is arguing that our conviction of this truth is "intuitively certain," rooted in the "law of our nature," and not, as Hume believes, the result of our observation and experience, the point is not how we arrive at our conviction but whether this conviction is sufficient warrant for assuming that the cause of the universe bears an evident resemblance to the Christian concept of God. But Beattie evidently thinks he has cut the ground from under Hume's position once he has proved to his own satisfaction that men cannot *help* but think that as "the universe had a beginning, it must have had a cause." At least, it is only at the very end of his chapter that he devotes a few words to the central point at issue.[36] And here he simply assumes, as obvious to common sense, that "when we take a view of the universe, and its parts, as of works curiously adapted to certain ends," we see that "their frame proves the cause to be intelligent, good, and wise;" and to the difficulty posed by Hume's remark concerning "the reality of that evil and disorder with which the world so abounds," Beattie is content to refer his readers to the "first part" of Butler's *Analogy* as a sufficient answer to this and other of Hume's "cavils" against the "divine attributes."

There seems no reason to believe that Beattie consciously misrepresents Hume's position. The great success of his book is due in part no doubt to the fact that his readers wished to be convinced. But Beattie's misunderstandings of Hume indicate the strength of traditional patterns of thought. Beattie does not escape these patterns; they are so much a part of him that he can hardly *think* as Hume thinks.

One is haunted by Johnson's statement in 1763 that "Every thing which Hume has advanced against Christianity had passed through my mind long before he wrote" (I, 444). It is true that by 1763 all of Hume's writings on religion had appeared with the sole exception of the *Dialogues*. And the *Dialogues*, brilliant as they are, propound no criticism of religion which could not have been gathered, by inference at least, from Hume's earlier writings. But in view of Johnson's endorsement of Beattie, we cannot take this statement at face value. Johnson—in print at least—never comes to grips with Hume's fundamental critique of religion.

Before leaving this subject we should note a general consideration Johnson advances against "Hume and other sceptical innovators" in religion. It is derived from Johnson's view of civilization as a vast cooperative enterprise depending upon the contributions of many minds. "A system," he tells us, "built upon the discoveries of a great many minds, is always of more strength, than what is produced by the mere workings of any one mind, which, of itself, can do little." Johnson is not thinking of Hume specifically here but he immediately goes on to apply the principle to Christianity, arguing that "there is a balance in its favour from the number of great men who have been convinced of its truth, after a serious consideration of the question" (I, 454). We recall Johnson's statement that Christianity "must be received upon conviction, and successively received by those whom conviction reached." Johnson never shared Hume's view of the Christian centuries as a vast desert of ignorance and superstition. The man who sprinkled the pages of his *Dictionary* with citations from Hooker, who in turn sprinkled *his* pages with citations from the Church Fathers, believed there were men of understanding and intelligence in every age.[36a] And Johnson assumes that if such men were "successively" convinced of the truth of Christianity, such conviction inevitably involved some inquiry into the validity of the evidences. Thus Johnson conceives of these as having been tested and weighed through the centuries. And so there is a sense in which he considers Christianity itself as a system, not "built upon" but *confirmed by* "the discoveries of a great many minds." It is this high valuation of the cumulative weight of testimony that lies behind Johnson's outburst against Hume as "a man who has so much conceit as to tell all mankind that they have been bubbled for ages, and he is the wise man who sees better than they" (V, 29). It is a case of one mind against many minds, and for Johnson, "the mere workings of any one mind . . . can do little."

This is, I think, Johnson's "ultimate" argument, the one he would have invoked had he recognized the strength of Hume's critique of the Design and First Cause arguments. Hume's critique, he might have said, seems watertight; yet it is the product of one mind opposing itself to the conclusions of many minds, and these are not to be regarded a priori as less acute than Hume's. When Johnson remarked that everything Hume had advanced against Christianity had passed through his own mind, he added:

> Always remember this, that after a system is well settled upon positive evidence, a few partial objections ought not to shake it. The human mind is so limited, that it cannot take in all the parts of a subject, so that there may be objections raised against any thing. There are objections against a *plenum*, and objections against a *vacuum*; yet one of them must certainly be true. (I, 444)

It is easier to believe, Johnson might have said, that Hume has erred—although the error may not be easily apparent—than to believe that all mankind "have been bubbled for ages,"[37] especially when one considers that Hume's mind, as well as those of his critics, is "limited."

I cannot give an informed account of present-day Catholic opinion on this matter, but among many Protestant theologians "it is now widely acknowledged," as one of them writes, "that the a priori path to a proof of divine existence has been blocked by Kant's criticism of the Ontological Argument, while the various a posteriori routes have been fatally undermined by Hume's attack upon the Argument from (or to) Design." And so many Christians today are left with "a theology without proofs," a situation for which David Hume (by himself and through his influence on Kant) is in part responsible. Hume has won the battle; what of the war? If one judges by the interest shown in theology today and by the number of theological works written, it may seem that the theology without proofs is doing reasonably well, a situation which, I suspect, would have been deplored—for very different reasons—by both Samuel Johnson and David Hume. But Johnson, if he could have reconciled himself to it, would have understood the current religious situation better than Hume. As Professor John Hick goes on to say, for a theology without proofs, "the central epistemological problem becomes that of the nature of faith"[38]—and faith Johnson knew about, but faith in the religious sense Hume never understood.

Professor J. H. Randall, Jr., believes it by no means clear that Hume in the essay on miracles was not sincere in stating, "Our most holy religion is founded on faith, not on reason."[39] If Hume was sincere, one might interpret this to mean that Hume accepted the *legitimacy* of a theology without proofs; that he understood, and had no quarrel with, the Christian concept of faith. Hume then, according to this view, is merely angry at the attempt to found religion on reason, but he has no quarrel, whatever his own beliefs, with those theologians who would ground it upon faith, bypassing what Hume considers the vain attempt to support it through argument and "evidences." But I cannot think Hume would have written so many pages demonstrating, often with the keenest irony, the total irrationality of religious beliefs, if he had not thought this procedure effective in disposing of any conceivable justification for religion. Basil Willey is surely right when he remarks that Hume, having "established that Christianity is founded on Faith, not on Reason . . . feels that he has disposed of it."[40]

I pointed out earlier in this chapter that although Johnson believes Christianity "reasonable," he is not a Christian because he finds the evidences "irresistible." In the next chapter I want to consider the appeal which orthodoxy had for Johnson in a more positive sense; that is, I want to explain why I think it difficult to imagine Johnson *other* than orthodox.

Ethics and Eschatology

IT IS QUITE POSSIBLE, as W. J. Bate and Robert Voitle have shown, to discuss Johnson's ethical theory apart from his religious views. Starting from the premise that God has designed man for society, Johnson is able to consider the matter simply from the point of view of what actions contribute most to the happiness of men as social beings. The public good, considered from a secular, this-worldly point of view, is the goal aimed at; and Johnson's criteria for determining whether an action is good or bad are derived from its results: does the action tend to increase or diminish the "sum of human happiness"? Thus Voitle can argue plausibly that Johnson's ethical theory strongly resembles that of Richard Cumberland, who has been called the "founder of English Utilitarianism."[1]

But—one must immediately add—it turns out on examination that those acts which contribute most to the happiness of society are precisely those acts of charity and benevolence demanded by religion. Johnson finds no incompatibility between the New Testament ethic and the ethic of social utility. To "do unto others as ye would have them do unto you" is a religious commandment. The Christian who ignores it places his eternal happiness in jeopardy.[2] But for Johnson this commandment also points to a rule of life which, if generally practiced, would greatly increase the "sum of happiness" of any society, Christian or non-Christian.

Thus, in Sermon 5, Johnson argues that God originally

created man "for happiness" *in this world.* "The Fall" changed all that, but men may still do much to promote their happiness in this life, and to effect this, "no miracle is required; men need only unite their endeavours, and exert those abilities which God has conferred upon them, in conformity to the laws of religion." If this were done, "even our present state may be made pleasing and desirable," and Johnson points out the practical advantages that would ensue: the alleviation of poverty, for instance. Emphasizing public as well as private happiness, he remarks that

> a community, in which virtue should generally prevail . . . would be opulent without luxury, and powerful without faction: its counsels would be steady, because they would be just; and its efforts vigorous, because they would be united. The governours would have nothing to fear from the turbulence of the people, nor the people any thing to apprehend from the ambition of their governours. The encroachments of foreign enemies, they could not always avoid, but would certainly repulse; for scarce any civilized nation has been ever enslaved, till it was first corrupted.[3]

This is far indeed from the Mandevillean assumption that private vices are public benefits.[3a] Far from weakening the material prosperity and political power of the state, the general practice of the Christian virtues, as Johnson sees it, would tend to establish both the prosperity and the power upon a just and equitable basis.

But the phrase "Christian virtues" is misleading. Johnson does not really acknowledge two sets of virtues, the Christian and the non-Christian. We have noted one apparent exception to this statement. Johnson does believe that Christian charity differs *in kind* from types of benevolence known to the ancient world. But it differs, not as a virtue sharply *opposed* to its nearest analogues in pagan and non-Christian religions; it is, rather, a further refinement and rectification of a virtue which men who have never heard of the Christian revelation may know and practice. To be sure, the rectification is vastly important, so much so that what we have is something really new, different in kind from any of its non-Christian analogues. Such an interpretation seems in harmony with Johnson's criticism of the "philosophers of the heathen world." He calls their notions of virtue "narrow," but not wrong-headed or perverse.[4]

It is true also that Johnson believes revelation has brought into the world moral precepts of greater "purity" than any known before (IV, 124), but here again it is a matter of degree, of rectification, not a matter of one set of virtues replacing another radically different set. When the Duc de Chaulnes said "that the morality of the different religions existing in the world was nearly the same," Johnson did not deny it. He merely added—a very important addition, to be sure—"that the Christian religion alone puts [morality] upon its proper basis—the fear and love of God."[5] In general, the great value of revelation for Johnson, so far as its bearing on morality is concerned, is not that it brings into the world an ethic wholly unknown before, nor an ethic sharply in opposition to non-Christian ethical systems, but rather that it strengthens men in the practice of virtues already known. Its doctrines, especially the doctrine of the Atonement, make it abundantly clear to all men how greatly God loves virtue and abhors vice (IV, 124). What before was a matter of speculation, of "philosophy," is now plainly revealed by God himself. It is Christian eschatology, not the greater purity of Christian ethics, which is the *primary* service of revelation to morality. Christianity, putting morality upon its proper basis, the fear of Hell and the hope of Heaven, has provided the strongest of all possible motives for the practice of virtue.

Thus Johnson, speculating on the morality of the ancient world, finds "no reason to wonder, that many enormities should prevail where there was nothing to oppose them." The ancients, with no certain knowledge that virtue would be rewarded or vice punished in a future state, lived in a world where it was only to be expected that some men would please themselves whenever they could "with very little regard to the rights of others." And so Johnson concludes that "notwithstanding all the securities of the law, and all the vigilance of magistrates," the state of the ancient world must have been a state of "disorder; a state of perpetual contest for the goods of this life, and by consequence of perpetual danger to those who abounded, and of temptation to those that were in want."[6]

It must be remembered that when Johnson considers the ethical thought of antiquity he thinks of it as "philosophy," the product of human, not divine, wisdom. The official polytheistic religion of ancient Greece and Rome is simply mythology as far as Johnson is concerned, and while he knows that some ancients were theists, that some believed in an afterlife and had other eschatological notions, he regards this development as a natural result of the fact that men in all ages are able by the light of reason and nature to make more or less plausible inferences concerning the nature of God. But Johnson does *not* believe that God intervened in any way to enlighten the philosophers of the ancient world as to his true nature, except insofar as he endows some men in every age with greater powers of mind than others. Johnson acknowledges only two genuine revelations of the divine nature—the Mosaic and the Christian. He is aware of non-Christian religions, of Judaism, and of Mohammedanism in particular, which last he considers the only serious rival to Christianity in his own day (IV, 199). All of these—Judaism, Christianity, and Mohammedanism—are religions of the "Book," all of them have their prophets, and all lay claim to a divine revelation. Thus, whether true or false, they are for Johnson religions, not philosophies.

But the eschatological ideas of the ancients, however refined, did not pretend to be anything more than the products of human wisdom. Since the eschatological problem had been solved by Christianity, Johnson is little interested, except as a matter of curiosity, in what antiquity has to say on the subject. Moreover, eschatology can never advance further than speculation. Men, by taking thought, can never learn anything absolutely certain about a realm of being not amenable to sense experience. Only a divine revelation can show whether their speculations, however reasonable, are true or false, and the philosophers of antiquity laid no claim to such a revelation.

But the case is otherwise with ethics. As we have seen, Johnson makes no radical distinction between Christian and non-Christian ethical systems. All men are moralists by necessity; all are constantly faced with problems requiring moral choice. Ethical ideas, unlike eschatological speculations, can be tested by experience. Experience may determine whether or not they "work," whether or not they add to or lessen the "sum of human happiness." The interest which the ethical ideas of antiquity had for Johnson, and the reason why his thoughts on the subject are of interest today, is that he saw in the "heathen philosophers" a sustained attempt—the only such attempt known to him—to present a secular, this-worldly solution to those problems of existence for which Christianity offers a supernatural, other-worldly solution. For Johnson the ideas of these philosophers represent the supreme instance of what the unaided reason of man can do—and cannot do—in coping with the manifold problems of this earthly life.

Certain types of classical philosophy held little interest for Johnson. All forms of hedonism, of carpe diem philosophizing, seem to Johnson so inadequate as a means of coping with the harsh realities of existence that he hardly thinks them worth refuting. The grosser forms of hedonistic indulgence, in which the "mind" has no part, are briefly disposed of in *Rasselas*, chapter 17. As for the more refined forms of hedonism, Johnson has no quarrel with any man who advocates the pursuit of "rational" pleasures, but when such pursuit is raised to the level of "philosophy," when it becomes a way of life, it breaks down at just that point where any creed or philosophy must prove its worth—it has nothing to say when calamity strikes. This point is crucial. Johnson has no use for any creed or philosophy unless it makes some provision, not for the minor misfortunes of everyday life, but for those major calamities which afflict every man sooner or later.

In ancient stoicism Johnson encountered a philosophy fully aware of the calamitous nature of human existence. One reason why there are so many references to stoicism in Johnson's writings is simply that he found the stoics "in his way," so to speak. No one who has read far in Johnson will have failed to see how often he offers advice in coping with the miseries of life. As he puts it at the beginning of *Rambler* 32: "So large a part of human life passes in a state contrary to our natural desires, that one of the principal topicks of moral instruction is the art of bearing calamities." And the stoics had addressed themselves to just this problem. Johnson had read widely in the writings of the ancient stoics; he was also well acquainted with the *De Constantia* of the Renaissance writer Justus Lipsius, whom he calls "the great modern master of the stoick philosophy."[7]

Johnson has no fundamental quarrel with the moral precepts of stoicism. Like the stoics, he admires courage and fortitude, and, generally speaking, what the stoic writers agree to call "virtue" Johnson is willing to accept as such. His basic criticism of stoicism is simply this—that it doesn't work.

Commenting on the "art of bearing calamities," Johnson remarks that

> The sect of ancient philosophers, that boasted to have carried this necessary science to the highest perfection, were the stoicks, or scholars of Zeno, whose wild enthusiastick virtue pretended to an exemption from the sensibilities of unenlightened mortals, and who proclaimed themselves exalted, by the doctrines of their sect, above the reach of those miseries which imbitter life to the rest of the world. They, therefore, removed pain, poverty, loss of friends, exile, and violent death, from the catalogue of evils; and passed, in their haughty style, a kind of irreversible decree, by which they forbade them to be counted any longer among the objects of terrour or anxiety, or to give any disturbance to the tranquillity of a wise man.

For Johnson the stoic attempt to overcome the ills of life through philosophy is doomed to failure. The experience of "every hour" shows that the arts of reason and philosophy can only palliate, they can never cure, that "infelicity" which is "involved in corporeal nature, and interwoven with our being."[8]

Even religion itself can be no more than "palliative" so

far as the evils of this life are concerned. But in the Christian doctrine of a future state of "compensation" Johnson finds what is for him a rational solution to the problem of evil. Johnson can accept a number of the stoic prescriptions for alleviating the less serious misfortunes of life. He can agree with Lipsius and the "common voice of the multitude" that our fortitude in the face of adversity is strengthened if we pause to consider how others every day are facing worse calamities; he can agree with Seneca that all misfortune is not absolutely evil and therefore to be avoided at all costs, for "to escape misfortune is to want instruction, and . . . to live at ease is to live in ignorance."[9] But the great test of stoicism, as of any secular ethic, is the consolation it provides in the face of death, that greatest of all calamities. It is, after all, the death of his daughter that effectively shatters the philosophic defenses of the stoic sage in *Rasselas*.

The best single statement of Johnson's attitude occurs in *Idler* 41 where Johnson, deeply moved by the death of his mother a week earlier, describes what is for him the only possible consolation in such a case. Here, if anywhere, Johnson speaks from the heart. "Other evils," he says, "fortitude may repel, or hope may mitigate," but the death of one dear to us is "irreparable privation," leaving "nothing to exercise resolution or flatter expectation. The dead cannot return, and nothing is left us here but languishment and grief." Surely, then,

> there is no man who, thus afflicted, does not seek succour in the Gospel, which has brought "life and immortality to light." The precepts of Epicurus, who teaches us to endure what the laws of the universe make necessary, may silence but not content us. The dictates of Zeno, who commands us to look with indifference on external things, may dispose us to conceal our sorrow, but cannot assuage it. Real alleviation of the loss of friends, and rational tranquillity in the prospect of our own dissolution, can be received only from the promises of him in whose hands are life and death, and from the assurance of another and better state, in which all tears will be

wiped from the eyes, and the whole soul shall be filled with joy. Philosophy may infuse stubbornness, but religion only can give patience.

The teachings of the stoics, however useful in alleviating the ills of this life, are useless when we face the prospect of leaving it. The stoics promise more than they can perform. They claim to inculcate a "rational tranquillity" at the prospect of death—our own or that of someone dear to us—but at best they can teach us only to conceal that anguish which considerations based merely on *human* wisdom ("philosophy") can never eradicate. Compared to this, the hope of the Christian is eminently "rational" because belief in the gospel promise of eternal happiness can really "assuage" our grief on such occasions and, as Johnson points out, revelation does not forbid us to hope "that the union of souls may still remain; and that we who are struggling with sin, sorrow, and infirmities, may have our part in the attention and kindness of those who have finished their course and are now receiving their reward."

This is the statement of a man who was, as J. W. Krutch has said, "a pessimist with an enormous zest for living."[10] And that zest for living found its greatest solace and keenest delight in social intercourse, in human ties and affections, in the mutual intercourse of "mind with mind." This is why Johnson is suspicious of any ethic which attempts to fortify us against disappointment by counseling an attitude of cautious reserve, if not outright indifference, in our relations with others. Don't get involved, runs the assumption, then as now, and you won't get hurt. The "dictates of Zeno" and those of the stoic sage in *Rasselas* are intended "to keep our minds always suspended in such indifference, that we may change the objects about us without emotion." But, says Johnson, although "an exact compliance with this rule might, perhaps, contribute to tranquillity . . . surely it would never produce happiness. He that regards none so much as to be afraid of losing them, must live for ever without the gentle pleasures of sympathy and confidence; he must feel no melting fondness, no warmth of benevolence, nor any of those honest joys which nature annexes to the power of pleasing." And so Johnson concludes that the "attempt to preserve life in a state of neutrality and indifference, is unreasonable and vain." Vain because "misery will find its way at many inlets" whatever we may do to fortify ourselves against it; unreasonable because it can never be reasonable "not to gain happiness for fear of losing it."[11] Thus, even as a means of coping with ills less serious than death, stoicism, in Johnson's view, manifests its inadequacy. If it gives a measure of tranquillity, it does so at the expense of a greater good, happiness.

Again, says Johnson, "it has been the boast of some swelling moralists, that every man's fortune was in his own power, that prudence supplied the place of all other divinities, and that happiness is the unfailing consequence of virtue." To be sure, if every man were virtuous, it would mean greater—but not unlimited—happiness for all. This is the argument of Sermon 5, but failing the attainment of this earthly Utopia, Johnson cannot believe that virtue is necessarily its own reward in this life. On the contrary, "the quiver of Omnipotence is stored with arrows, against which the shield of human virtue, however adamantine it has been boasted, is held up in vain: we do not always suffer by our crimes; we are not always protected by our innocence." This fact is one of the strongest "moral arguments for a future state; for since the common events of the present life happen alike to the good and bad, it follows from the justice of the Supreme Being, that there must be another state of existence, in which a just retribution shall be made, and every man shall be happy and miserable according to his works."[12] The goal which the stoics and other secular moralists seek to attain is a worthy one, it may even represent "heights of wisdom"—but it is unattainable: "It was the boast of the Stoick philosophy, to make man unshaken by calamity, and unelated by success, incorruptible by pleasure, and invulnerable by pain; these are heights of wisdom which none ever attained, and to which few can aspire."[13]

Thus for Johnson the virtues of the stoic are founded on an unwarranted pride in human self-sufficiency. This kind of pride is a sin in Christian theology, for no one can be a Christian who believes man is sufficient unto himself, but here again revelation and human experience teach the same lesson. As Johnson says in Sermon 3, "the philosophers of the heathen world seemed to hope, that man might be flattered into virtue, and therefore told him much of his rank, and of the meanness of degeneracy; they asserted, indeed with truth, that all greatness was in the practice of virtue; but of virtue their notions were narrow, and pride, which their doctrine made its chief support, was not of power sufficient to struggle with sense or passion."[14]

It is clear what the "chief support" of virtue must be. Man is *not* self-sufficient. Only in the Christian promise of "life and immortality" does he find motives to virtue sufficient to support him in his lifelong struggle with "sense or passion." And in the daily practice of the Christian life, in public and private devotion, these motives are continually brought to mind, strengthened, and renewed.

There has been a good deal of speculation as to what Johnson would have become had he "let himself go." He was so much the sceptic in worldly matters, he so often gives the impression, as Hogarth puts it, that he is resolved to believe nothing *but* the Bible,[15] that some critics have seen in Johnson a temperament more inclined to scepticism and free thought than to religious faith. Johnson's faith came hard for him, so runs this assumption, and his notorious fear of death is thus the product of "insecure faith" and its consequence, "a terror of annihilation." This view has been generally abandoned, at least by those who have made a special study of Johnson's religious outlook. Johnson so often couples his fear of death with his fear of judgment, especially in his later years, that it is difficult to see in this anything other than a perfectly orthodox faith in a future state of rewards and punishments. The intensity of his fear is thus a measure of the intensity of his faith, not a sign that this faith is "insecure." Thus many scholars today would agree with Robert Voitle who sees in Johnson a man with a "temperament emotionally disposed to religion." And Voitle opposes Johnson's "agony" to the "assurance" of the freethinker: "All men may be compounded of opposites, yet the trait most characteristic of the temperament genuinely disposed to freethinking is assurance, not agony."[16]

But if there is agony for Johnson there is also hope, a hope which makes the agony bearable. Let me go back a little here to consider the whole question of Johnson's pessimism. It is not that Johnson experiences life and finds it dross. Quite the contrary; he lives it to the hilt, extracting every bit of enjoyment from it that he can. But he wants *more* enjoyment, always more, and his imagination, restless, active, and powerful beyond that of most men, continually suggests possibilities of happiness which his reason—equally powerful—assures him can never be attained. And so again and again Johnson returns to the limited, frustrating nature of earthly existence as an argument for a future state where man, that being "capable of enjoying so much more than is here to be enjoyed"[17] will at last find enjoyments equal to his capacity.

What we have here is what Miguel de Unamuno has called "the hunger of immortality."[18] In Johnson's case it stems directly from that enormous zest for living of which Krutch speaks. It flows from his enormous vitality, his love of existence for its own sake. He would rather exist in pain than not exist at all (III, 296). "Protracted existence," he tells us (IV, 374), "is a good recompence for very considerable degrees of torture," and "no wise man will be contented to die if he thinks he is to fall into annihilation."[19] "Protracted existence" is what Johnson wants, existence protracted beyond the grave. His fear of being found unworthy at the Last Day is very real and very powerful, but it is, logically, a secondary consideration. What Johnson wants in the first instance is personal immortality, life without end, forever and ever. His fear of judgment is the reverse side of the coin. He knows there are conditions attached, and that not every man who cries "Lord, Lord" will be received into the kingdom of "life and immortality." Thus I cannot believe that Johnson would have found any comfort whatever in any religion or philosophy that rejected or left in doubt the possibility of an afterlife. Had Johnson "let himself go," it would not have been in the direction of scepticism or free thought but in the direction of what his contemporaries called "superstition." Had not his "stubborn rationality" interposed, he might have become a Roman Catholic or he might have persuaded himself that the Cock Lane Ghost was a veritable manifestation of "spirit."

Thus those who argue that Johnson had a terror of annihilation are right. But if it is possible to speak of a temperament emotionally disposed to religion, this terror, positively expressed as a hunger for immortality, is surely a distinguishing mark of such a temperament. Certainly, the true secularist knows nothing of it. It is, of course, only one distinguishing mark; many devout Christians whose faith is less troubled than Johnson's may never have had it. They accept the eschatology of their religion but they are, by temperament, people whose serene confidence in the gospel promises of an afterlife could never be accurately described by the phrase "hunger of immortality." Nevertheless, some men in all ages *have* had this hunger, and Unamuno, whether we call him a Christian or not, is a notable modern instance. His book *The Tragic Sense of Life* reveals very clearly the dilemma of the modern man who must believe in an afterlife ("I need it in order to live," he tells us)[20] but who is convinced that reason gives no grounds for such a belief.

It may seem that I am multiplying causes in excess of necessity. All we really know is that Johnson feared death because he feared judgment—the evidence is quite clear on this point. The few texts indicating Johnson's fear of annihilation are slim evidence in themselves for assuming a positive "hunger of immortality." Thus it may be argued that Johnson's fear of death is adequately explained by Professor Quinlan, who tells us that it was based "upon strong doubts about his own merits."[21] To be sure it was—at the conscious level. But I am trying to get behind this level to indicate why I believe orthodoxy, although Johnson admitted it was somewhat "strange" to reason (I, 398), was nevertheless the only possible faith for a man of his temperament. Of all available alternatives in his own day, only orthodoxy held out the positive hope of "life and immortality," and I would argue that this was, for Johnson, its compelling attraction, whether he was consciously aware of it or not.

Unamuno argues that the desire for personal immortality is a sign of life, health, and vitality: "Only the feeble resign themselves to final death and substitute some other desire for the longing for personal immortality. In the strong the zeal for perpetuity overrides the doubt of realizing it, and their superabundance of life overflows upon the other side of death." This statement seems to me almost wholly wrong as a generalization but almost wholly accurate as a description of Johnson's own case.[22] With Johnson it is indeed a "superabundance of life" overflowing "upon the other side of death" that makes it impossible to imagine him other than an orthodox believer in life after death. As Professor Quinlan rightly says, "Because sentience meant so much to him, [Johnson] could not believe that anyone who had no faith in an afterlife could approach death with tranquillity."[23] Yes. But if we take into account those many passages in which Johnson stresses the frustrating, unsatisfactory nature of "sentience" itself, we may be led to see behind this criticism a positive hunger for eternal life. Not, certainly, for the eternal survival of sentience as we know it in this life. Johnson's horror at the idea of "immortal men" matches that of Swift.[24] But for Johnson man in this world is but "half man," as it were. His "faculties," his very senses, too often serve but for his torment. Johnson envisions the afterlife as that condition where man becomes *fully* man, where he becomes capable at last of enjoyments equal to his capacity. He may need to be endowed by God with *new* faculties suitable to his altered state, but this in no way changes matters. His altered state is his *true* state. In a very real and very literal sense Johnson conceives of personal immortality as the state man—at least fallen man—is *born* to. God has so managed matters that only in the afterlife can man find that self-fulfillment which stoics and other secularists claim he may achieve, in some measure at least, in this life. But for Johnson, any self-fulfillment which man *can* achieve in this life is not enough. Johnson can always imagine something much better, and what he can imagine his religion tells him he may achieve.

It is not, then, its ethic, which is for Johnson the supreme fact about Christianity. What he values is the eschatology, that above all else. Those Christian "mysteries," so great a stumbling block for the sceptical intellect in the eighteenth century, are for Johnson the sine qua non of his religious faith. Unamuno, talking to a Spanish peasant one day, proposed the hypothesis that there might be a God who governs all things, but that nevertheless "the soul of every man may not be immortal in the traditional and concrete sense." The peasant replied, "Then wherefore God?"[25] Wherefore, indeed, Johnson might have said, unless He can provide men with a "rational hope" that this life is not all there is.

VII

Evil, Free Will, and "Necessity"

IT MIGHT BE SUPPOSED THAT A MAN as impressed as Johnson was with the evils of life might have been more than a little disturbed at the difficulty of reconciling the fact of evil with the perfections of the Deity. As Hume put it, "EPICURUS'S old questions are yet unanswered. Is GOD willing to prevent evil, but not able? then he is impotent. Is he able, but not willing? then he is malevolent. Is he both able and willing? whence then is evil?"[1] Johnson had given this matter considerable thought, but it is characteristic of him that when he thinks of the evils of life his *first* impulse is to turn this fact into an argument for a future state of "compensation." It is the practicing Christian in him which speaks first. He is always more interested in practical than in speculative theology. Boswell once "talked to him of original sin, in consequence of the fall of man, and of the Atonement made by our Saviour." After "some conversation," Johnson at Boswell's request dictated a lengthy statement of his views. Original sin Johnson dismisses in a brief first paragraph: "With respect to original sin, the inquiry is not necessary; for whatever is the cause of human corruption, men are evidently and confessedly so corrupt, that all the laws of heaven and earth are insufficient to restrain them from crimes" (IV, 123-24). The rest of Johnson's statement is devoted to the Atonement; that is, not to speculation concerning the origin of sin but to the practical matter of God's plan for saving men from its consequences.

Yet that Johnson had given serious thought to the problem of evil is clear from his review of Soame Jenyns' *Free Enquiry into The Nature and Origin of Evil*.[2] This review is one of the best things he ever wrote and the only sustained example from his pen of more or less strictly "philosophical" or "metaphysical" criticism. At the very beginning of his review, which appeared in 1757, Johnson points out that the problem of the nature and origin of evil can never be freed "from the perplexity which has entangled the speculatists of all ages, and which must always continue while *we see* but *in part*." Two years later, in *Idler* 89, he gives what I take to be a definitive statement of his considered opinion: "How evil came into the world; for what reason it is that life is overspread with such boundless varieties of misery; why the only thinking being of this globe is doomed to think merely to be wretched, and to pass his time from youth to age in fearing or in suffering calamities, is a question which philosophers have long asked, and which philosophy could never answer." The problem, then, is not amenable to any satisfactory solution, and I find no evidence that Johnson departed from this position in later life. From his cogent discussion of the issues in the Jenyns review, and from his reference to "the speculatists of all ages," I think it safe to assume that he had long since concluded that the best philosophers can do is to present more or less likely hypotheses, no one of which can ever be regarded as definitive.

In *Idler* 89 Johnson demonstrates his own faith in the Christian answer. "Religion informs us," he says, "that misery and sin were produced together," and the remainder of this essay develops the proposition that "almost all the moral good which is left among us, is the apparent effect of physical evil." The fear of disease checks the progress of vice, the fear of retaliation checks the progress of injustice, and "of charity it is superfluous to observe, that it could have no place if there were no want."

As to Jenyns' "chain of being" theory and the consequence he draws from it, that partial evil is universal good— Johnson never denies that evil may be in some sense necessary to the production of good. The trouble is that "as far as human eyes can judge, the degree of evil may have been less, without any impediment to good" (p. 48). Pointing out that "the scale of existence, from infinity to nothing, cannot possibly have being," Johnson indicates his sense of the utter gratuitousness of existence so far as human reason can explain it: "since, on the one side, creation, wherever it stops, must stop infinitely below infinity, and on the other, infinitely above nothing, what necessity there is, that it should proceed so far, either way, that beings so high or so low [as men] should ever have existed? We may ask; but, I believe, no created wisdom can give an adequate answer" (pp. 52-53). The utterly gratuitous nature of the universe itself is one reason why existential evil is not to be ascribed to God. Johnson quotes with approval the following passage from Jenyns: "Whatever we enjoy, is purely a free gift from our creator; but, that we enjoy no more, can never, sure, be deemed an injury, or a just reason to question his infinite benevolence. All our happiness is owing to his goodness; but, that it is no greater, is owing only to ourselves; that is, to our not having any inherent right to any happiness, or even to any existence at all." As Johnson says, these sentiments are not new, but he quotes them because they are important "and may be read, with pleasure, in the thousandth repetition" (p. 49). Johnson does not share the belief, current in some theological circles today, that man is in some sense necessary to God. Johnson holds to the traditional orthodox belief that God is wholly self-sufficient; that the gift of existence is wholly gratuitous, a work of supererogation, as it were.

This, for Johnson, is a powerful argument in favor of the goodness of God against all complaints of existential evil. Life with all its pains is so much better than nonlife that complaints of evil fade in importance by comparison with this primal good. Johnson, unlike Jenyns, is never tempted to argue that *any* aspect of existence is other than gratuitous. Given the world as it is, it is possible to make sense out of it, but Johnson is always conscious of the fact that there might have been no world at all or that it might have been a very different kind of world. Thus, when Jenyns defends poverty as necessary but then goes on to say that God might easily have excused men from labor, since at God's command "the earth would readily have poured forth all her treasures," Johnson remarks that

> if God *could easily have excused us from labour*, I do not comprehend why he *could not possibly have exempted* all from poverty. For poverty, in its easier and more tolerable degree, is little more than necessity of labour; and, in its more severe and deplorable state, little more than inability for labour. To be poor is to work for others, or to want the succour of others, without work. And the same exuberant fertility, which would make work unnecessary, might make poverty impossible (pp. 60-61).

When Johnson remarks that Jenyns has said nothing of religion but what he has learned or might have learned from the divines, that it is not universal, that it is obscure, that its evidences are not irresistible, he goes on to agree with Jenyns that the corruptions of religion are to be ascribed to men rather than to religion itself. Johnson then adds the significant remark: "All this is known, and all this is true; but why, we have not yet discovered" (p. 75). From the existential point of view, Christianity itself is utterly gratuitous; we cannot tell why it *exists*, any more than we can tell why we ourselves exist.

As no man can tell why God chose to create man, so no man can tell why the quantum of moral and "physical" evil in the world is as great as it is. Jenyns is guilty of presumption, of "dogmatical limitations of omnipotence" (p. 63). The assumption of a chain of being is a limitation of God's omnipotence not only because Jenyns presumes to say (without, as Johnson sees it, any warrant from reason or revelation) that God effects his will through such a metaphysical structure and no other, but also because the tendency of Jenyns' argument is to imply that God *could* have effected his will in no other way.

Johnson distrusted anything that smacked of moral determinism. In his review of Jenyns we see his distrust of anything which seems to limit God's omnipotence. But God's omnipotence involves, if not moral determinism, at least a foreknowledge of all that occurs, for God cannot be supposed ignorant of future events. If men's actions, including those of moral value, are not "caused" by God they are at least "foreseen" by Him. Johnson reacts to the free will problem much as he reacted to Berkeley's immaterialism: "We *know* our will is free, and *there's* an end on't" (II, 82). In spite of such dogmatism, there is evidence that Johnson had given serious consideration to the free will problem just as he had to problems of theodicy. The two problems are intimately related, for if every act of moral value is strictly "determined" it is difficult to see how such acts can be judged good or bad. Boswell once remarked that he thought "predestination, or what is equivalent to it, cannot be avoided, if we hold an universal prescience in the Deity":

> Johnson. 'Why, Sir, does not God every day see things going on without preventing them? Boswell. 'True, Sir; but if a thing be *certainly* foreseen, it must be fixed, and cannot happen otherwise; and if we apply this consideration to the human mind, there is no free will, nor do I see how prayer can be of any avail.' He mentioned Dr. Clarke, and Bishop Bramhall on Liberty and Necessity, and bid me read South's Sermons on Prayer; but avoided the question which has excruciated philosophers and divines, beyond any other. (II, 104)

Since Johnson himself never presents a systematic defense of free will, it will be appropriate to consider what South, Bramhall, and Clarke have to say about it. Although Robert South does not address himself directly to the free will problem, it is easy to see why Johnson recommended his sermons on prayer to Boswell. South's view of prayer is carefully consistent with a full recognition of God's "universal prescience" and omnipotence. In the first of two sermons "Against Long Extemporary Prayers," South indicates why prayer is not to be regarded as an invasion of God's omniscience. South points out first of all that prayer prevails with God *not* by way of information, persuasion, or importunity. To allow that it does prevail in these ways would be to admit that God is not omniscient, that he does not know our thoughts "before the very heart that conceives them," and that, like men, he is moved by "passion or affection," or is capable of being wearied "into a concession of what we beg of him."[3] South is aware of Biblical texts which seem to indicate that God *is* moved to grant men's prayers "by way of importunity or persuasion" or "by fervency or earnestness" (p. 244). His answer is that such texts speak anthropomorphically, "according to the manner of men; and consequently, ought to be understood only of the effect or issue of such prayers, in the success certainly attending them, and not of the manner of their efficiency" (p. 245). Prayer then, for South, prevails with God

> neither by way of information, nor yet of persuasion, and much less by the importunity of him who prays, and least of all by any worth in the prayer itself, equal to the thing prayed for; but it prevails solely upon this account, that it is freely appointed by God as the stated, allowed condition, upon which he will dispense his blessings to mankind. (p. 243)

South then asks why prayer "rather than any other thing, comes to be appointed by God for this condition" (p. 243). His answer indicates the importance South attached to prayer as one of the most fundamental obligations—and one of the greatest privileges—of the Christian life. God has appointed prayer as the "allowed condition" for the dispensation of his blessings because prayer is "most eminently and properly an act of dependence upon God." To the reply that the wicked who do not pray are also dependent upon God, South points out that prayer is voluntary, an act of "moral dependence," a recognition of the fact that the person praying is not sufficient unto himself. Associated with "the highest reverence of God," prayer is opposed to all types of irreverence:

"forasmuch in every irreverent act, a man treats God as if he had no need of him, and behaves himself as if he stood upon his own bottom, absolute and self-sufficient" (p. 245). Prayer for Johnson, as for South, is the great sign of our dependence upon God. It is, as Johnson says in Sermon 3, "the great efficient of union, between the soul and its Creator . . . of which the necessity is such, that St. Paul directs us, to pray without ceasing; that is, to preserve in the mind such a constant dependence upon God, and such a constant desire of his assistance, as may be equivalent to constant prayer."[4]

Johnson, I believe, would have endorsed South's explanation of prayer as I have summarized it here. Certainly he would wish, like South, to regard the efficacy of prayer as wholly consistent with God's universal prescience. But Boswell, interpreting "universal prescience" in a strict deterministic sense, wonders how man can be said to have free will if all his actions have been "*certainly* foreseen" by God. Boswell's question is debated in what Johnson calls "Bishop Bramhall on Liberty and Necessity." Johnson is referring to the classic seventeenth-century discussion of the free will problem, portions of which are still reprinted.[5] In 1646 Thomas Hobbes had written a treatise "Of Liberty and Necessity" in reply to a manuscript on the same subject by John Bramhall, Bishop of Derry. In 1655 Bramhall printed his own manuscript together with Hobbes's as *A Defense of True Liberty From Antecedent and Exstrinsical Necessity*. The following year Hobbes printed Bramhall's treatise along with his own detailed replies as *The Questions Concerning Liberty, Necessity, and Chance*. In the Bramhall book, as in that of Hobbes, the separate manuscript treatises of the two men are broken down into sections of "argument and reply" loosely organized around a particular argumentative crux. Hobbes, of course, defends "necessity"; Bramhall argues stoutly for the freedom of the will. Samuel Clarke, coming later in time, is aware of the Hobbes-Bramhall controversy, and very conscious in his *Demonstration* of the need to refute Hobbes on the free will issue. His full title indicates this: "A Demonstration of the *Being* and *Attributes* of God. More Particularly in Answer to Mr. Hobbes, Spinoza, and their Followers. Wherein the Notion of Liberty is Stated, and the Possibility and Certainty of it Proved, in opposition to *Necessity* and *Fate*."

The first conclusion I would like to draw concerns Johnson's knowledge of Hobbes. There are very few Johnsonian references to Hobbes in Boswell or in Johnson's writings. But it seems clear that Johnson was well acquainted with Hobbes's writings and that he was thoroughly aware of the destructive nature of Hobbes's materialistic determinism so far as religion is concerned. The "argument and reply" arrangement of the debate as published means that Johnson could not have read Bramhall without reading Hobbes. Moreover, in the *Dictionary* Johnson cites "Bramhall against Hobbs" at least three times under terms pertinent to the free will controversy (twice under "necessitation," once under "reprobation"), and the sale catalog of his library lists the complete Dublin edition of Bramhall's works (item 214). And in Clarke's *Demonstration* quotations from Hobbes sprinkle the margins and Hobbes's arguments are frequently referred to and summarized in the text.

As to the debate itself, both Hobbes and Bramhall agree that God has absolute foreknowledge. From this, Hobbes argues "that all things are necessary [i.e., determined], since if they were not, some of the things which God foreknew might not come to pass, and 'the prescience of God is quite taken away.' " For Bramhall's view I can do no better than to quote Professor Mintz's summary. For Bramhall,

'the knowledge of God comprehends all times in a point, by reason of the eminence and virtue of its infinite perfection.' From man's vantage point this type of knowledge must be called foreknowledge, but for God it is actually a knowledge of past, present and future comprehended simultaneously. This means that God's knowledge of any future event does not depend on his knowledge of that event's antecedent causes, and hence necessity cannot be inferred from foreknowledge. 'God did know that Judas should betray Christ; but Judas was not necessitated to be a traitor by God's knowledge. If Judas had not betrayed Christ, then God had not foreknown that Judas should betray him.' God foreknows every thing, but in matters affecting human volition, the determining agent is man's own unfettered will. God knows what choices man will make, but he has left man free to choose.

This is a traditional Christian view, shared alike by the Puritan Milton and the Royalist Bramhall.[6] Clarke adds nothing of substance to Bramhall, but his argument, unimpeded by the interruption of the debate form, is easier to follow. Clarke, pointing out that God himself must have free will, asks why God may not determine that the will of man should also be free.[7] Johnson makes the same point in a citation from Hammond under "predetermination": "This *predetermination* of God's own will is so far from being the determining of ours, that it is distinctly the contrary; for supposing God to predetermine that I shall act freely; 'tis as certain from thence, that my will is free in respect of God, and not predetermined." Insisting that foreknowledge does not imply necessity, Clarke admits that "the *Manner* how God can foresee Future things, without a Chain of Necessary Causes; is impossible for us to explain *distinctly*." But he goes on to argue that we can get some general notion of it, for a man who knows another person well, although he has no influence over that person's actions, "can yet often perceive before-hand what That Other will do . . . So 'tis very reasonable to apprehend, that *God,* without influencing Mens Wills by his Power, yet by his Foresight cannot but have as much *Certainer* a knowledge of future free Events, than either Men or Angels can possibly have; as the *Perfection* of *His* Nature is greater than that of *Theirs*."[8] Johnson uses the same argument on one of those few occasions when Boswell was able to draw him out on this subject: "If I am well acquainted with a man, I can judge with great probability how he will act in any case, without his being restrained by my judging. God may have this probability increased to certainty" (III, 291).

But does Johnson believe that his own arguments or those

of Bramhall, Clarke, or Hammond are conclusive? Apparently not. "All theory," he tells us, "is against the freedom of the will; all experience for it." This is an astonishing statement. Bramhall was no unworthy opponent of Hobbes, and it would be difficult to maintain, even today, that *all* theory is against the freedom of the will. Other Christians, most notably T. S. Eliot, have believed that Bramhall got the better of Hobbes.[9] But not Johnson. On at least two occasions in 1769 Boswell queried Johnson on the free will problem. Johnson refused to give his opinion, although on the second occasion he gave Boswell the references I have discussed here. Later, in 1778, Boswell did manage to discover what Johnson himself thought.

What is chiefly of interest in this 1778 discussion is the fact that Boswell—against his will—scores a clear victory over Johnson. In 1769, noting Johnson's refusal to commit himself, Boswell had advanced the opinion that Johnson *could* have solved the free will problem if his "supposed orthodoxy" had not "cramped the vigorous powers of his understanding" (II, 104). In 1778 Boswell, pushing the case for "necessity," does manage to elicit a few Johnsonian remarks in defense of free will—each one of which Boswell shoots down—and then comes Johnson's capitulation: "All theory is against freedom of the will; all experience for it." Boswell, happy to have got Johnson to say this much, "did not push the subject any farther" (III, 290-91).

Professor Pottle's recent biography indicates how much Boswell was bothered by the free will problem.[10] But Johnson could not have solved it for him. Johnson is perfectly willing to recommend authorities to Boswell—and to the readers of his *Dictionary*—who write in defense of free will. He hopes their arguments will convince others, but they have not convinced *him*, and that, I believe, was why he was reluctant to discuss the matter with Boswell in 1769. Let Boswell read the authorities without prejudice. Perhaps he would find their arguments more convincing than Johnson had found them.

Certainly Johnson wanted to be convinced that theory as well as experience was on the side of free will. If he was not, it may be that his reading of Hobbes was chiefly responsible. Bramhall was a good reasoner, but Hobbes, after all, was one of the great minds of the seventeenth century, and his side of the controversy with Bramhall "was written with exceptional clarity and dialectical rigour."[11] But we should also note an obvious fact—the progress of science since the days of Hobbes and Bramhall. Looked at from one point of view, Newton's great discoveries simply added scientific confirmation to what Hobbes had earlier maintained—that the universe is a "Great Machine, working by rigidly determined laws of material causation."[12] Thus it may be that Johnson, realizing this, was more impressed than Hobbes's seventeenth-century opponents with the question Hobbes puts to the orthodox: Why, if "necessity" rules in nature, should man, who is a part of nature, constitute an exception to the general rule?

Nevertheless, Johnson believes in free will. The pertinent distinction here between Johnson and Hobbes is that Hobbes believes theory takes precedence over experience, that a cogent train of reasoning is always proof against an appeal to "feeling." Hobbes is aware that men "feel" they are free, but this counts as nothing against Hobbes's faith in the cogency of his argument. Thus Hobbes can admit that we are ignorant in many instances of the factors that determine us to take this or that action; nevertheless all our actions are strictly "necessitated" even if we are utterly ignorant of the causal sequence that determines them. But for Johnson experience takes precedence over theory: "You are surer that you are free, than you are of prescience; you are surer that you can lift up your finger or not as you please, than you are of any conclusion from a deduction of reasoning" (III, 290). For Johnson, if reason and experience conflict, it is reason which must give way. The fact that men *act* as though they were free agents is a sufficient answer to all theoretical objections: "But, Sir, as to the doctrine of Necessity, no man believes it. If a man should give me arguments that I do not see, though I could not answer them, should I believe that I do not see?" (IV, 329).

Johnson has a further argument which he opposes to the determinists. "Moral evil," he tells us, "is occasioned by free will, which implies choice between good and evil. With all the evil that there is, there is no man but would rather be a free agent, than a mere machine without the evil; and what is best for each individual, must be best for the whole. If a man would rather be a machine, I cannot argue with him. He is a different being from me" (V, 117). This is not merely an argument against deterministic theory but a defense of what for Johnson makes man distinctively human. Johnson is justified in putting the case in terms of extremes—man is "free" or he is a "machine"—for Hobbes's determinism is nothing if not rigorous. So also is that of such later writers as Holbach, whose *Système de la Nature* Johnson attacked (V, 47-48). I believe Boswell right in thinking that Johnson regards the doctrine of the freedom of the will in its theoretical aspects much as he regards the doctrine of the Trinity: it is reason but not contrary to it (IV, 329). We are sure that our will is free— God has "predetermined" that it should be—but we cannot answer all theoretical objections while we see "but in part."

VIII

Church and State

DONALD GREENE HAS DONE MUCH to clear Johnson of the charges of a bigoted Toryism in politics; he has shown indeed that Johnson's Toryism is often nearer allied to present-day liberal attitudes than to what we now think of as political conservatism. But there is one aspect of Johnson's thought which can hardly be called liberal—if liberalism includes adherence to the principle of separation of church and state. As Greene points out, Johnson was "a stout partisan of the Church of England, and of the maintenance of its position in the state." And Greene is surely right when he says this loyalty to the Church, more than any other of Johnson's political feelings, "can be confidently said never to have wavered throughout his adult life." It is no part of Greene's purpose to examine this loyalty in detail: he explains it simply in terms of Johnson's Lichfield background. It was a political characteristic Johnson "had in common with Midland squires and country parsons."[1]

Yet this loyalty is worth examining because Johnson's support of the privileged position of the Church in English life shapes several of his most conservative, not to say illiberal attitudes. "Liberal" Johnson certainly was in several of the noblest and most spacious meanings of that honorable term; antilibertarian he certainly was, also, if we measure his convictions against current attitudes. Johnson could have accepted that part of the First Amendment to the U.S. Constitution which allows for the right of the people "peaceably to assemble

118

and to petition the Government for a redress of grievances," but he did *not* believe the legislature should "make no law respecting an establishment of religion," and he supported laws and practices which liberals today would certainly regard as prohibiting the free exercise of religion and limiting freedom of speech and of the press.

Johnson all his adult life held the position he ascribes to Swift: "he desired the prosperity and maintained the honour of the Clergy; of the Dissenters he did not wish to infringe the toleration, but he opposed their encroachments."[2] The "toleration" of which Johnson speaks is the Toleration Act of 1689. Given legal recognition by this act, the dissenters were no longer subject to persecution on the ground of treasonable activity. While it would not be accurate to say that the dissenters from 1660 to 1689 had no legal rights which an Anglican was bound to respect, it is true that for most of this period "the persecution of non-conformists was the official policy of England's rulers."[3] Not so after 1689. The evident futility of the persecution policy, the ardent support given the Revolution by the sects, and the growth of the latitudinarian spirit combined to effect a widespread change in public sentiment. The old persecuting spirit, revived under Anne, was finally laid to rest under Walpole. After the accession of George I the *toleration* of dissent was no longer an issue in English politics.

But if the dissenters were now recognized as citizens, entitled to the protection of the laws, theirs was distinctly a second-class citizenship. Chief among their legal disabilities was the Test Act. Originally directed against Roman Catholics, this act required all officeholders, "civil or military," to produce written evidence that they had received "the sacrament of the Lord's Supper according to the usage of the Church of England." This provision effectively barred conscientious dissenters, as well as Catholics, from important political office, and thus from positions of trust and responsibility in the state. As a result in part of such laws, the dissenters throughout the eighteenth century "were consigned to a backwater of the national life." Resenting this discrimination, especially in view of their staunch support of the Hanoverian dynasty, the dissenters and their allies in parliament made many attempts to improve their position—all without success. Indeed, G. R. Cragg can write that "in some respects the position of the dissenters actually deteriorated" as the century wore on.[4] Except for isolated instances, there was no active persecution, and there were many mitigations of the laws in practice, but what I am concerned to stress here is simply the fact of discrimination as by law established—and the fact that Johnson approves it. In the *Life of Swift* Johnson remarks that "the reasonableness of a Test is not hard to be proved; but perhaps it must be allowed that the proper test has not been chosen." This means, I think, that Johnson would have agreed with Lord Eldon who "never desired to retain the sacramental test, if any other equivalent security could be substituted."[5] But the "equivalent security" was not found, and so Johnson continued to support a sacramental test, although admitting that this *form* of test was less than "proper." Certainly, Johnson regarded the bills periodically introduced in Parliament "for the relief of the Protestant Dissenters" not as acts of simple justice to an inoffensive minority but as acts of "encroachment" against the rightful authority of the Church. Johnson stands foursquare for the "toleration": beyond that he refuses to go.

In this Johnson was at one with the nation as a whole. The dissenters could always count upon the sympathy and active support of a number of Whigs and Churchmen of strong liberal and latitudinarian principles, but such groups were never strong enough, numerically or otherwise, to overcome the general conviction that no further concessions should be made to dissent.

At the same time, some Anglicans found it rather difficult to justify their position. G. M. Trevelyan, speaking of the events of 1689, remarks that at this time, "Thanks to Holland and England, religious *toleration* began to have a place in the practice and thought of Europe. But religious *equality* was an idea that existed neither in the laws of European States nor in the minds of men."[6] Whatever the situation in 1689, the idea of religious equality was common enough in eighteenth-century England. There were those who came to believe that the peculiar privileges of the national church "could no longer be defended."[7] And Anglicans out of sympathy with this view felt impelled at least to defend their position—often at great length. It is true that violent all-out attacks on the very idea of an established church are rare before the time of Paine, but the books, tracts, and parliamentary proposals that formed the basis of popular discussion left no doubt in anyone's mind that the question at issue was that of equality, in fact if not in name. The Church might remain "established" in law and in custom, but if all the measures proposed by its eighteenth-century critics had been adopted, the Church's relation to other Protestant groups could hardly have been much more than primus inter pares.

Johnson never offers a systematic presentation of his own position on this matter, but his scattered remarks give us a fairly clear conception of his views. It seems clear from these remarks that what Johnson opposes is not so much the idea of equality per se as the belief that such an ideal could ever be attained in practice. Properly qualified, Trevelyan's remark *does* apply to Johnson and to a very large segment of Anglican opinion. The idea of religious equality was familiar; what was *not* familiar was the idea that religious groups could live together in a state of legal equality without constant attempts at "encroachment" upon one another's freedoms. It was assumed that if non-Anglicans had access to positions of power in the state, they would inevitably use this power against the Church. As Anglicans saw it, the Puritans had done precisely that during the Interregnum, the Catholics during the reign of James II, and who could guarantee, if the discriminatory laws were repealed, that the dissenters, favored by the early Hanoverians, would not succeed where these others had—ultimately —failed? Few Anglicans were willing to risk the experiment. They could and did argue that theirs was a position not selfish merely; what was good for the Church was good for society as a whole, including dissenters. Given the assumption that religious sects are by nature antagonistic to one another; given the further assumption that religious strife is one of the worst evils that can befall a nation—it then followed that any system which reduced the possibility of such strife was justified, especially since the dissenters now merely suffered discrimination, not the persecution that their ancestors had inflicted upon Anglicans in the preceding century. Indeed, as G. R. Cragg points out, there was some irritation at "the insufficient gratitude of the nonconformists." They should not complain, it was felt, of the "few and reasonable limitations" placed upon them.[8]

How, according to the Anglican view, did such discrimination preserve the peace and ensure the stability of the social order? Since the dissenters regarded the Test Act as especially unjust, while many Anglicans saw it as indispensable for the safety of church and state, most Anglican arguments may be fairly described as defenses of "an established religion and a test law." Of these the best known, then and now, was William Warburton's *The Alliance Between Church and State* (1736), written at a time when "orthodox nonconformists, in the not unnatural belief that their steady support of the House of Hanover and the Whig Party deserved to be rewarded, were carrying on an agitation for the repeal of the Test Act." *The Alliance Between Church and State*, which first brought Warburton into notice, was still regarded well into the nineteenth century "as a treatise which had to be taken into serious account."[9] Johnson, we know, was a sincere, although by no means uncritical, admirer of Warburton's writings. I find no indication that he had read Warburton's *Alliance* treatise, but it is safe to say that he was familiar with Warburton's argument since he *had* read and enjoyed Warburton's masterpiece, *The Divine Legation of Moses* (1737, 1741), and the argument of the *Alliance* treatise is repeated in the later work.[10] I make no claim that Johnson was influenced by Warburton's views, although there are interesting similarities. But a summary of certain parts of Warburton's systematic argument may help to clarify Johnson's scattered pronouncements on the same subject.

Warburton is at great pains to avoid the charge that he advocates a theory of religious persecution or even that he is defending the privileged position of the Church of England as such. "His only aim," as A. W. Evans says, "is to show that an established church of some sort is necessary for the well-being of a community and that there is no injustice in excluding from political influence all those who do not conform to its doctrines whatever these doctrines may be."[11] If one assumes, as Johnson and Warburton do, that religion is of the utmost importance to the individual since nothing can be more important to any man than a knowledge of those things necessary for salvation, it follows that the state should do nothing to hinder the free exercise of religion, since the state exists to promote the welfare of its citizens, and by the law of nature, as Warburton says, "every man hath a right of worshipping God according to his own conscience."[12] Theoretically, as Warburton admits, the great ends of religion could be attained without any sort of visible church, but human nature being what it is, the stability and continuity of religion cannot be assured without a professed creed and public ritual. The essence of religion is the "commerce" of the individual with his God,[13] but the weaknesses of human nature make it necessary that believers, for their mutual protection and support, should organize themselves into religious societies. The invisible church of the spirit must have its counterpart in some sort of external organization. But granted the necessity of a visible church, why an *established* church? Why should the state find it necessary to discriminate in favor of one religious group as against all others? Warburton's answer is based upon his understanding of history. As Warburton sees it, it is the *nature* of religious groups to encroach upon one another—at least that has been true in the past and Warburton finds no reason to believe it will be less true in the future:

> For amongst diversities of sects, where every one thinks itself the *only true*, or at least, the *most pure*, every one aims at rising on the ruins of the rest; which it calls, *bringing into conformity* with itself. The means of doing this, when reason fails, which is rarely at hand, and more rarely heard when it is, will be by getting into the public administration, and applying the civil power to the work.

> But, when one of these Religions is the *established*, and
> the rest under a *toleration;* then envy, at the advantages
> of an *establishment*, will join the *tolerated churches* in
> confederacy against it, and unite them in one common
> quarrel to disturb its quiet. In this imminent danger, the
> *allied* [i.e. the established] *church* calls upon the State,
> for the performance of its contract; which thereupon
> gives her a TEST-LAW for her security: whereby, the
> entrance into the Administration of public affairs (the
> only way, the threatened mischief is effected) is shut to
> all but members of the *established church*.[14]

The established church should be that of the majority of
the people, and if ever the majority declines to a minority,
the state should disestablish the minority religion in favor of
the prevailing creed. Thus, the situation whereby Anglicanism
was established in England and Presbyterianism in Scotland was
for Warburton no anomaly but an eminently just and reasonable arrangement. Warburton assumes that the established
church, favored by the majority and secure in its privileges,
will have no desire to persecute minority sects: its posture will
be purely defensive.[15]

Warburton also assumes that religious strife is to be
avoided at all hazards. Allowing for the spirit of reason and
compromise, he considers it too weak—at least in matters of
religion—to be relied upon to preserve the peace where "diver-
sities of sects" coexist. Searching history, he finds that "an
ESTABLISHED RELIGION WITH A TEST-LAW" has
proved the best solution to the problem, that it is, in fact,
"the universal voice of Nature": "the most savage nations
have employed it to civilize their manners: and the politest
knew no other way to prevent their return to barbarity and
violence."[16]

In comparing Johnson's views with Warburton's we may
note once again Johnson's hatred of any form of religious
persecution. "The rancour and hatred," he tells us, "the rage
and persecution, with which religious disputes have filled the
world, need not to be related; every history can inform us,

that no malice is so fierce, so cruel, and implacable, as that which is excited by religious discord." Or again: "All violence, beyond the necessity of self-defence, is incited by the desire of humbling the opponent, and, whenever it is applied to the decision of religious questions, aims at conquest, rather than conversion."[17] Had Johnson considered the laws which "established" the Church as a species of "violence" against dissenters, he would never have countenanced them.

And Johnson, like Warburton, admits that the great ends of religion could be achieved without the aid of a visible church. Indeed, he gives us an example. John Milton had not "associated himself with any denomination of Protestants . . . . he was not of the church of Rome; he was not of the church of England," and yet there is no doubt in Johnson's mind that Milton, surly republican though he might be, was a sincere and orthodox Christian (he was "untainted by any heretical peculiarity of opinion"). But Johnson agrees with Warburton that the visible church is a practical necessity. In spite of Milton, "to be of no church is dangerous" because "religion, of which the rewards are distant and which is animated only by Faith and Hope, will glide by degrees out of the mind unless it be invigorated and reimpressed by external ordinances, by stated calls to worship, and the salutary influence of example." Johnson never forgot that period when religion had "dropped" out of his own mind, and his experience of life reinforced his conviction that what had happened to him was no unusual occurrence. A man like Milton "whose studies and meditations were an habitual prayer" was in no danger of neglecting religion, but the great majority of men, who remain "in a kind of equipoise between good and ill," need to be constantly reminded of their eternal as against their worldly interest, and this reminder the visible church exists to provide in the form of external ordinances, stated calls to worship, and "the salutary influence of example."[18]

But Johnson, supporting the status quo, is not willing to consider the "visible" congregations of dissent as on a par with those of the Church. Johnson knew and esteemed many dissenters as individuals, and for some—Baxter and Watts, for instance—he had the highest admiration. But whatever the merits of dissenters as individuals, it is clear that when Johnson thinks of the sects in a collective sense, he sees them, like Warburton, as the *natural* enemies of the Church. Thus, defending the exclusion of dissenters from the universities, he remarks that, as the universities "were founded to bring up members for the Church of England . . . we must not supply our enemies with arms from our arsenal" (II, 151). In 1773 a measure was proposed to relieve dissenting ministers from the obligation, imposed by the Toleration Act, of subscribing to the greater part of the Thirty-nine Articles. It is probably with reference to this proposal that Johnson, writing to an Anglican clergyman, remarks with evident satisfaction that "Opposition seems to despond; and the dissenters, though they have taken advantage of unsettled times, and a government much enfeebled, seem not likely to gain any immunities" (II, 208, n. 4). (Edmund Burke, it is interesting to note, took the more liberal view; he supported the measure.)[19]

But if there is to be an established church, privileged as the Church of England is privileged, Johnson agrees with Warburton that this church should be that of the majority of the people. As against the sixteenth-century principle that the people should adopt the religion of their sovereign, Johnson believes it natural and just that the religion of the majority should become the established religion of the country, with whatever authority in law may be necessary to ensure its preservation against sects inimical to it. It is on these grounds that he defends the expulsion of James II. Here it was a case of the majority rightfully defending itself against a then powerful minority. In eighteenth-century Ireland the case was just the reverse, and Johnson was highly indignant: "The Irish," he said, "are in a most unnatural state; for we see there the minority prevailing over the majority. There is no instance, even in the ten persecutions, of such severity as that which the Protestants of Ireland have exercised against the Catholicks" (II, 255).

The logic of Johnson's position becomes clear when we turn to consider his attitude toward the religious developments of the seventeenth century. As far as the history of Great Britain was concerned, it had been the sects chiefly, Johnson thought, not the Anglicans, who had displayed that spirit of "rancour and hatred" which he associates with religious discord. And so he can speak of "the sullen superstition, the gloomy moroseness, and the stubborn scruples of the ancient Puritans" and, with reference to John Knox, of the "malignant influence of calvinism."[20] Johnson does not confuse seventeenth-century Puritanism with eighteenth-century dissent, but he does believe that if the spirit of religious fanaticism were to reappear, it would come, not from the powerless Catholic minority,[21] but from the more numerous dissenters or, if not from the older dissenting bodies, from newly established sects full of the zeal and enthusiasm which always animate converts to a new religion. In either case, such fanaticism would derive from a social and economic background closely associated in Johnson's mind with both seventeenth-century Puritanism and eighteenth-century nonconformity. Thus, in *The False Alarm* (1770) Johnson associates dissent with pro-Wilkes agitation, remarking contemptuously that it is no wonder Wilkes "has been supported by the sectaries, the natural fomentors of sedition, and confederates of the rabble, of whose religion little now remains but hatred of establishments, and who are angry to find separation now only tolerated, which was once rewarded." *The False Alarm* is Johnson at his most intemperate, but I find no indication that he would have repudiated this statement in his cooler moments. It seems clear from the context that the last clause refers to the Interregnum, and Johnson's remark that little now remains of dissenting religion except hatred of establishments is a biased recognition of the fact that the religious fervor of the "ancient Puritans" had declined remarkably among their eighteenth-century descendants. The drift of Presbyterian orthodoxy toward Arianism, Socinianism, and ultimately Unitarianism was sufficiently noticeable by 1770, and for Johnson anti-Trinitarianism is "heresy" and hence in his more polemical moments "loss" of religion.[22] Certainly, in *The False Alarm* Johnson's irritation gets the better of his sense of fairness. "Hatred" is not the word to describe the attitude of most dissenters toward the Church in 1770, and Johnson could hardly be ignorant of the decline in *numbers* of the dissenting congregations, a fact much discussed in his own day and confirmed by modern historians. How, then, did nonconformity pose a threat to church or state?

For Johnson one of the most dangerous consequences of seventeenth-century Puritanism had been its encouragement of the "rabble." The democratic overtones of the Puritan ethic—its heavy emphasis on the right of private judgment in matters of religion—was, as Johnson clearly saw, a major factor in the proliferation of new sects during the Interregnum. When Johnson abuses the "sectaries" of his own day as the "natural fomentors of sedition, and confederates of the rabble," he has in mind the social chaos of the preceding century. There had been a time when the "vulgar" had been a power in the land, and the experiment, Johnson thought, had not been a happy one. "It is scarcely possible, in the regularity and composure of the present time," he writes,

> to imagine the tumult of absurdity and clamour of contradiction which perplexed doctrine, disordered practice, and disturbed both publick and private quiet in that age, when subordination was broken, and awe was hissed away; when any unsettled innovator who could hatch a half-formed notion produced it to the publick; when every man might become a preacher, and almost every preacher could collect a congregation.

One of the ends of government, as Johnson saw it, was the preservation and transmission to posterity of the values of civilized society. And experience had shown that these values were not safely entrusted to the common people. Thus, while "the wisdom of the nation is very reasonably supposed to reside in the parliament," "what can be concluded of the lower classes of the people," Johnson asks, "when in one of the parliaments summoned by Cromwell it was seriously proposed that all the records in the Tower should be burnt, that all memory of things past should be effaced, and that the whole system of life should commence anew?"[23]

Johnson wished well to the common people but he had no faith in their political or religious wisdom. Boswell once teased him with an account of the infidelity of his servant who would not believe the Scriptures because he could not read them in their original tongues, and be sure they were not invented. "Why, foolish fellow," said Johnson, "has he any better authority for almost every thing that he believes?" Boswell: "Then the vulgar, Sir, never can know they are right, but must submit themselves to the learned?" Johnson: "To be sure, Sir. The vulgar are the children of the State, and must be taught like children" (II, 14).[23a]

What Johnson feared is well illustrated in the case of Edward Elwall (1676-1744), a religious eccentric who was tried and acquitted in 1726 on charges of having written a book against the Trinity. Elwall wrote an account of his trial in which he boasted that he had "challeng'd the greatest Potentates on earth; yea, even the King of Great Britain, whose true and faithful Subject I am, in all temporal things, and whom I love and honour: Also, his noble and valiant Friend, John Argyle, and his great Friends Robert Walpole, Charles Wager, and Arthur Onslow; all these can speak well, and who is like them; and yet, behold, none of all these car'd to engage with their Friend Elwall." Johnson's account of Elwall is worth transcribing in full:

> Sir, Mr. Elwal was, I think, an ironmonger at Wolverhampton [according to the *DNB* he was a mercer and grocer by trade]; and he had a mind to make himself famous, by being the founder of a new sect, which he wished much should be called *Elwallians*. He held, that everything in the Old Testament that was not typical, was to be of perpetual observance, and so he wore a ribband in the plaits of his coat, and he also wore a beard. I remember I had the honour of dining in company with Mr. Elwal. There was one Barter, a miller, who wrote against him; and so you had the controversy between Mr. ELWAL and Mr. BARTER. To try to make himself distinguished, he wrote a letter to King George the Second, challenging him to dispute with him, in which he

said, "George, if you be afraid to come by yourself, to dispute with a poor old man, you may bring a thousand of your *black*-guards with you; and if you should still be afraid, you may bring a thousand of your *red*-guards."

But, Johnson concludes, "Mr. Elwal failed in his scheme of making himself a man of great consequence" (II, 164, n.4).

This account is humorous enough; obviously poor Elwall posed no threat to church or state. But he *might* have, and the Church in alliance with the state had every right to protect society against the possibility of future, more successful Elwalls. Elwall was certainly "unsettled" in his religious views: he was "successively a unitarian, a churchman, and an Ebionite" (*DNB*). Worse than that from Johnson's point of view, he had attempted to convert others to his views; he had attempted to found a sect. Johnson's contempt for Elwall's learning is sufficiently evident; Elwall is for Johnson just that sort of half-educated "unsettled innovator" in religion who in the preceding century had done so much to disturb "publick and private quiet."

Certainly Johnson feared nothing from the respectable dissenting orthodoxy of a Watts or a Baxter; what he feared was the ethos of dissent itself, and he found no reason to believe *this* had changed since the days of Cromwell. For Johnson that ethos, overstressing the right of private judgment in religion, was far more likely to give rise to unsettled innovators like Elwall than the more conservative Anglican ethos.[23b]

For Johnson all civilized nations were composed of two sorts of people—the illiterate or semiliterate masses and the educated elite. This distinction, or rather the interpretation he places upon it, explains the limitations Johnson would place upon freedom of speech and other freedoms of expression. These limitations have been often discussed in assessments of Johnson's social and political attitudes; the intimate connection they have with Johnson's religious outlook has been little noticed. But when Johnson condemns "unbounded" freedom of speech or of the press, he very often has in mind the dissemination of unorthodox opinions in religion. Thus, while religious speculation and difference of opinion among the educated is permissible and indeed necessary, Johnson believes the religious controversies of the learned should never be allowed to unsettle the orthodoxy of the masses. When asked whether he would restrain private conversation, Johnson replied: "Why, Sir, it is difficult to say where private conversation begins, and where it ends. If we three were to discuss even the great question concerning the existence of a Supreme Being by ourselves, we should not be restrained; for that would be to put an end to all improvement. But if we should discuss it in the presence of ten boarding-school girls, and as many boys, I think the magistrate would do well to put us in the stocks, to finish the debate there" (IV, 216).

As with private conversation, so with public oratory. Because the masses could only be effectively reached through the spoken word, the sermon in the eighteenth century could be a powerful factor in molding public opinion. The effect it could have is amply illustrated in the history of Methodism. One must have in mind the effect of pulpit oratory among "the lower classes of the people" when considering the limits Johnson places on freedom of speech. Because the Methodists were orthodox in point of doctrine, Johnson could occasionally commend their preaching as especially suited to the understandings of the common people. But he would have opposed any attempt to preach unorthodox doctrine, and by this he meant doctrine contrary to that taught by the Church of England. When Bennet Langton asked him whether it might not be "politick" for the magistrate to tolerate those who preached against the doctrine of the Trinity, Johnson replied that in his opinion it was *not* politic "to tolerate in such a case" because "permitting men to preach any opinion contrary to the doctrine of the established church, tends, in a certain degree, to lessen the authority of the church, and consequently to lessen the influence of religion" (II, 254).

So far as the printed word is concerned, the same principle applies. Johnson is aware of the dangers of censorship. In his comments on Milton's *Areopagitica* he remarks on the danger of "unbounded liberty" of the press and the danger of "bounding it" as "a problem in the science of Government, which human understanding seems hitherto unable to solve. If nothing may be published but what civil authority shall have previously approved, power must always be the standard of truth," but if there is no restraint whatever, the effect, in Johnson's view, will be equally undesirable: "if every dreamer of innovations may propagate his projects, there can be no settlement; if every murmurer at government may diffuse discontent, there can be no peace; and if every sceptick in theology may teach his follies, there can be no religion."[24] Johnson has no faith in Milton's principle that in the conflict of opinions truth will vanquish error. Here again the experience of the seventeenth century is pertinent. As Johnson saw it, truth *had* lost to error. Moreover, whatever measure of truth or justice the Puritan cause might boast, the violent means they employed were destructive of the ends they sought to attain. For Johnson it is peace and social stability which best serve the cause of truth; indeed, for him these are the preconditions of any worthwhile society, and men must sacrifice something of their liberty to attain them.

Johnson may seem to place little faith in the strength of religious conviction when he says there can be no religion if every sceptic is free to teach his follies. But again it is with sceptics as with innovators in religion; Johnson sees them as *teaching* their scepticism, and, as most men are incapable of distinguishing with due care between error and truth, sceptical opinions, if widely disseminated, might certainly tend to lessen the influence of religion. As we have seen, Johnson was always impressed with the fragile hold religion has over most men. As he remarks in Sermon 10, "to live religiously, is to walk, not by sight, but by faith; to act in confidence of things unseen, in hope of future recompense, and in fear of future punishment. To abstract the thoughts from things spiritual is not difficult; things future do not obtrude themselves upon the senses, and therefore easily give way to external objects. He that is willing to forget religion may quickly lose it; and that most men are willing to forget it, experience informs us."[25]

The sceptic in theology is to be feared because he pretends to give men good reasons for "forgetting" something they are only too willing to forget in the natural course of events.

In 1773 Boswell asked Johnson "if it was not strange that government should permit so many infidel writings to pass without censure." Johnson thought it "mighty foolish" but explained it as a result of the political situation. The Hanoverians, opposed by the Church, encouraged the Whigs, and it is among Whigs that one finds men of "loose notions" in religion, with the result that since the Hanoverian succession, "there is no instance of any man being kept back on account of his bad principles; and hence this inundation of impiety" (V, 271-72).

The Licensing Act, which forbade the printing of any book without prior permission from a government censor, had expired in 1695 and was never reimposed. Johnson wanted no reimposition of the Licensing Act; indeed he specifically condemns this kind of legislation as making power the standard of truth.[25a] Nevertheless, it may be, as Edward A. Bloom thinks, that Johnson desired some kind of "restrictive laws before publication, to preclude the dangers of abuse."[26] But Johnson never tells us what sort of laws he desired, how they were to be framed, who was to administer them, what sort of books they were to be directed against, and so on. Perhaps he realized what a complicated and delicate task was involved, and was not clear in his own mind as to the solution of a problem which had hitherto baffled "the science of Government." To be sure, Johnson would like to see the civil power "censure" infidel writings, but this merely indicates his endorsement of current practice. The civil power did occasionally censure authors or printers of obnoxious books, and the censure varied from public burning of the book by act of parliament to fines levied upon author or printer or both, or—very rarely—to imprisonment. It is clear that Johnson thinks government lax in the use of censure, but nowhere does he advocate *new* laws to check the dissemination of "infidel" writings. One reason, I think, is that Johnson was not certain in his own mind as to the extent or influence of such writings. He could speak of an inundation of impiety, but he could also assert that "there is a great cry about infidelity; but there are, in reality, very few infidels" (II, 359). He may have relied upon time rather than the laws to effect a cure, as when he expressed the hope that "this gloom of infidelity . . . is only a transient cloud passing through the hemisphere, which will soon be dissipated, and the sun break forth with his usual splendour" (II, 81).

Reacting to a violent attack "against the Roman Catholicks," Johnson once chose to defend the Spanish Inquisition on the ground that "false doctrine should be checked on its first appearance" and that "the civil power should unite with the church in punishing those who dared attack the established religion, and that such only were punished by the Inquisition" (I, 465). The important thing here is that Johnson can defend the Inquisition only by maintaining that it punished those who actually *attacked* the established religion. This is essentially the same position he took with regard to the Church of England, and is consistent with his belief that the dissenters should be tolerated in the free exercise of their religion so long as they did not actively attack or otherwise attempt to undermine the religious faith or allegiance of the majority. So far from possessing the persecuting zeal of a Spanish Inquisitor, Johnson, in what he says on freedom of speech and of the press, is motivated by his fear of a revival in England of just such a spirit. Nowhere is this made clearer than in Sermon 23, perhaps the best single source for the matters dealt with in this chapter (see *Works* [1825], IX, 496-506).

This sermon, commemorating the death of King Charles I, is directed, as the Book of Common Prayer required, against "Disobedience and wilfull Rebellion," but is unusual in that Johnson does not choose for his text one of the many scriptural exhortations inculcating obedience to authority. Instead, from James 3:16 he chooses the text "where envying and strife is, there is confusion." Beginning with the statement that "the life of man is unhappy," a proposition which "requires no proof," Johnson considers this truth from the point of view of man "united in society," concluding that "in the prosecution of private interest, which providence has either ordained,

or permitted, there must necessarily be some kind of strife,"
but "this strife would be without confusion, if it were regu-
lated by reason and religion, if men would endeavour after
lawful ends by lawful means." The most dangerous kind of
strife is that which stems from difference of opinion in religion, and here Johnson, denouncing the spirit of persecuting
zeal, goes on to say that

> no man, whose reason is not darkened by some inordinate
> perturbation of mind, can possibly judge so absurdly of
> beings, partakers of the same nature with himself, as to
> imagine that any opinion can be recommended by cruelty
> and mischief, or that he, who cannot perceive the force
> of argument, will be more efficaciously instructed by
> penalties and tortures. The power of punishment is to
> silence, not to confute. It, therefore, can never serve for
> the effectual propagation, or obstruction, of doctrines.
> It may, indeed, sometimes hinder the dissemination of
> falsehood, and check the progress of errour, but can
> never promote the reception of truth.

Nothing could be further from Johnson's mind than any
inclination to see the civil power used as a means of stamping
out dissident religious denominations. His posture, like Warburton's, is purely defensive, and in his defense of the status
quo he is thinking as much of "society" as of the Church: "The
great benefit of society is that the weak are protected against
the strong. The great evil of confusion is that the world is
thrown into the hands, not of the best, but of the strongest;
that all certainty of possession or acquisition is destroyed; that
every man's care is confined to his own interest; and that general negligence of the general good makes way for general
licentiousness." ("Licentiousness" Johnson defines in the *Dictionary* as "boundless liberty, contempt of just restraint.") And
Johnson goes on to accuse the Puritans of having introduced
this confusion into the state: "Our laws were overruled, our
rights were abolished. The soldier seized upon the property,
the fanatick rushed into the church. The usurpers gave way
to other usurpers; the schismaticks were thrust out by other

schismaticks; the people felt nothing from their masters but alternatives of oppression, and heard nothing from their teachers but varieties of errour."

It was "the people" who suffered. It is not merely that the Puritans "church-outed" prelates of the establishment or that they murdered the king, when this was "not necessary, even to the safety of those by whom it was committed"— their greatest crime was not against individuals but against the people, the nation as a whole. As Johnson saw it, the Puritans in their revolutionary zeal had made it possible for a minority of the strong, the fanatical, the clever, and the unscrupulous to tyrannize over the majority, for

> in times of peace everything proceeds in a train of regularity, and hence there is no sudden advantage to be snatched, nor any unusual change of condition to be hoped. But when sedition and uproar have once silenced law, and confounded property, then is the hour when chance begins to predominate in the world, when every man may hope without bounds, and those who know how to improve the lucky moment, may gain in a day what no length of labour could have procured, without the concurrence of casual advantage.
>
> This is the expectation which makes some hasten on confusion, and others look with concern at its approach. But what is this other than gaining by universal misery, supplying by force the want of right, and rising to sudden elevation, by a sudden downfall of others?

The culmination of this "confusion" was that worst of all social evils, civil war,[27] "a war of the rabble against their superiors; a war, in which the lowest and basest of the people were encouraged by men a little higher than themselves, to lift their hands against their ecclesiastical and civil governours, and by which those who were grown impatient of obedience, endeavoured to obtain the power of commanding." As the Puritan leaders, men a "little higher" than the "lowest and basest of the people," encouraged the latter to revolt against their "governours," so Johnson in *The False Alarm* accuses the dissenters of doing precisely the same thing as "fomentors of sedition and confederates of the rabble" during the Wilkes agitation. The parallel is striking, and confirms one in the belief that the Wilkes affair is just the sort of "contemporary instance" which Johnson would have cited as justifying the retention in his own day of the privileged position of the Church—as against those who argued that the conditions which might have justified such privilege had long since passed away.

For Johnson the evils which beset the nation during the Interregnum were not past history merely. Behind all second causes stands God, the Cause of history itself, and so I think Johnson is not indulging merely in conventionally pious rhetoric when, near the end of his sermon, he mentions the evils of the Interregnum as a judgment "which God sometimes permits to fall upon nations, when they stand secure in their own greatness, and forget their dependence on universal sovreignty, depart from the laws of their Maker, corrupt the purity of his worship, or swerve from the truth of his revelation. Such evils surely we have too much reason to fear again, for we have no right to charge our ancestors with having provoked them by crimes greater than our own."

Johnson's attitude is a thoroughly pragmatic one. It derives ultimately from his view of human nature, especially of human nature seen on the stage of history, of British history in particular. Observation, experience, and history combine to show that man is capable of good but ever prone to pride, fanaticism of all sorts, and the ruthless pursuit of his own interest at the expense of his fellow man. As religion is the most important concern of man, so passions aroused by religious strife will be the most violent, the most potentially destructive of all human passions. When someone "praised the ancient philosophers for the candour and good humour with which those of different sects disputed with each other," Johnson replied that this was possible only "because they were not in earnest as to religion." They could dispute "with good humour upon their fanciful theories, because they were not interested in the truth of them: when a man has nothing to lose, he may be in a good humour with his opponent." And

Johnson lays it down as a principle that "every man who attacks my belief, diminishes in some degree my confidence in it, and therefore makes me uneasy; and I am angry with him who makes me uneasy. Those only who believed in Revelation have been angry at having their faith called in question; because they only had something upon which they could rest as matter of fact" (III, 10,11). Thus, although he deplores it, Johnson can understand the violence which accompanies disputes over religion: the English Civil War was fought for "a weighty and apparent interest. If the means were violent, the end was great. The civil war was fought for what each army called, and believed, the best religion and the best government."[28]

But now that the "best religion and the best government" had been reestablished, the question was how best to maintain it against a revival of such violence. Eighteenth-century defenses of the status quo in church and state often sound offensive today because so many of them are obviously motivated by class prejudice. Religion is discussed as though its most important function were to inculcate habits of obedience to authority among the "lower orders." Diverting their attention from the evils of their condition in this world to the hope of a heavenly utopia, religion serves to keep the masses quiet.

This kind of argument is wholly foreign to Johnson. Johnson wants social stability but he argues for it as in the best interests of every man, of whatever rank or class. And when Johnson thinks of "every man" he is thinking as much of his religious and moral as of his material well-being. For Johnson both James II and the Puritan leaders were, in a very real sense, enemies of the people. Introducing religious strife into the social order, they released destructive forces which were a threat to the *religious* well-being of every man in that order. The nonjurors, for example, excluded by their own "perverseness of integrity" "from the regular modes of profit and prosperity," were laid under "almost an irresistible temptation to be . . . criminal; for, a man *must* live, and if he precludes himself from the support furnished by the establishment, will probably be reduced to very wicked shifts to maintain himself."[29] Johnson might have added that if James II had not attempted to subvert the established order in church and state, the problem would never have arisen.

It is no exaggeration to say that Johnson has a *religious* horror of poverty. Poverty is dangerous to the welfare of the soul, as well for the souls of high-minded nonjurors as for those of the most illiterate day-laborers in the land. And this not only because the poor man is helpless to do good: he cannot help the needy and, although he may be wise, his "advice or admonition" will go unheeded since "few will reverence the understanding that is of so little advantage to its owner."[30] Thus, the poor man, tempted by his position "to mean arts and dishonorable shifts," is also hardly able to practice the great duty of Christian charity. As Johnson says in a letter to Boswell, "when the thoughts are extended to a future state, the present life seems hardly worthy of all those principles of conduct, and maxims of prudence, which one generation of men has transmitted to another; but upon a closer view, when it is perceived how much evil is produced, and how much good is impeded by embarrassment and distress, and how little room the expedients of poverty leave for the exercise of virtue; it grows manifest that the boundless importance of the next life, enforces some attention to the interests of this."[31]

Peace and social stability promote material well-being and alleviate poverty. When men are able to live in peace, freedom, and security, they possess the optimum material conditions for the effective practice of religion. Since government exists to promote these conditions, it must have the power to repress all disturbers of the peace. Because Johnson sees dissent as potentially a threat to peace and social stability, he supports the discriminatory laws. Because he regards the dissemination of unorthodox religious doctrine and "infidelity" as a threat, not merely to the social order, but to the religious "happiness" of all the people, especially the "vulgar," he would place limitations upon freedom of speech and the press.

Johnson's view is both conservative and liberal. It is conservative as against modern libertarian views in that it considers extensive or "unbounded liberty" in any area of human activity no necessary precondition of the good society; it is liberal in that its distrust of such liberty is based upon a sincere concern for the material and spiritual welfare of the common man, as against all invaders of his peace, security, and property. Johnson's view on liberty and its limits are those of a man who lacks faith in the possibility of any radical improvement of man's lot here on earth. The causes of man's unhappiness are rooted in his human nature, not in his environment. Since in Johnson's view there is relatively little that social or political change can do to mitigate this unhappiness, it follows that he looks elsewhere for a cure, insofar as a cure is possible. And he finds it in the Christian hope of a better world than this. Only the man who has this hope—who is not disturbed in the possession of it (by sceptics "in theology"), and not hindered in the practice of those virtues necessary to attain it (by social or religious disorder)—only this man is happy, insofar as happiness is possible here below.

Thus the limits Johnson would place on freedom of speech and action in any given case derive ultimately from his religion. His attitude in each instance is conditioned by what Hume called the "porch" view of human life, that is, by eschatology.[32] If Johnson thinks with horror of poverty and would do everything in his power to alleviate it (the "liberal" Johnson), it is not in the first instance because he has a kind heart but because he believes man has an immortal soul to save; if he thinks with equal horror of "infidelity" and would have it "censured" (the "reactionary" Johnson), it is for precisely the same reason.

IX

Johnson and the non-Christian World

IN JOHNSON'S DAY the factors that led to the great outburst of Christian missionary activity in the nineteenth century were not yet operative. So far as interdenominational proselytizing is concerned, Johnson, like most eighteenth-century Anglicans, hardly conceives of it as a recognized function of Christian sects. As Johnson sees it, civilized Europe is already Christian in the sense that all the major religions teach those truths necessary for salvation. I believe Johnson would have endorsed Mrs. Thrale's remark, "Why should Change of Sect be promoted among Xtians? We each of us do very well in our own: Let us all act up to what is taught us, and I see no Call for change." Let every man, Protestant or Catholic, faithfully practice the religion into which he is born, and all will be well. Nevertheless, Johnson does allow for change of sect under certain circumstances while Mrs. Thrale, more conservative in this respect, tends to regard all such conversions with a most suspicious eye. Johnson, for instance, welcomed the conversion of the Benedictine James Compton to Anglicanism; Mrs. Thrale thought this conversion set a bad precedent and believed the London clergy "right enough" in giving Compton "a very cold reception, and no Encouragement at all."[1]

But Johnson allowed for change of sect if it were the outcome of serious reflection by people mature enough and knowledgeable enough to know exactly what they were doing and why they were doing it. This was the case with Compton and with Johnson's friend John Walker, who converted from Presbyterianism to Catholicism.[2] It most emphatically was not the case, as Johnson saw it, with Miss Jane Harry, a convert from the Church of England to Quakerism. Young and ignorant, Miss Harry "could not have any proper conviction that it was her duty to change her religion" because, unlike Compton and Walker, she "knew no more of the Church which she left, and that which she embraced, than she did of the difference between the Copernican and Ptolemaick systems." And Johnson lays it down as a principle that

> we ought not, without very strong conviction indeed, to desert the religion in which we have been educated. That is the religion given you, the religion in which it may be said Providence has placed you. If you live conscientiously in that religion, you may be safe. But errour is dangerous indeed, if you err when you choose a religion for yourself. (III, 298-99)

There must be very strong conviction, and for Johnson no such conviction is possible for the unlearned, whether for the "vulgar," the children of the state, or for ignorant young women of the middle class like Miss Harry.

Johnson applies this principle consistently to members of non-Christian religions; he does not expect a "poor Turk" to be other than a Mohammedan (II, 14). But consideration of the non-Christian world raises the question of conversion in a more acute form because if Johnson believes there is little warrant for change of sect among Christians, since all major denominations are in possession of religious truth, he cannot believe the same of Mohammedanism, which is for Johnson the only truly formidable rival to Christianity on the world scene. Johnson does not share the belief, largely a product of nineteenth-century thought, that all the major world religions are more or less in possession of religious truth. Thus, with both Christianity and Islam in mind, Johnson remarks in his draft for *Irene* that "only one Religion can be true" (*Poems*, p. 359).

Johnson and the non-Christian World

Postponing for the moment consideration of Johnson's attitude toward Islam and other non-Christian religions, we may note that so far as the Christian world is concerned, Johnson manifests an active missionary zeal only where he encounters inexcusable pockets of ignorance. One of his most impassioned letters expresses his horror that anyone could oppose "the scheme of translating the holy scriptures into the Erse or Gaelick language, from political considerations of the disadvantage of keeping up the distinction between the Highlanders and the other inhabitants of North-Britain." "I did not expect to hear it could be," he writes,

> . . . a question whether any nation uninstructed in religion should receive instruction; or whether that instruction should be imparted to them by a translation of the holy books into their own language. If obedience to the will of God be necessary to happiness, and knowledge of his will be necessary to obedience, I know not how he that with-holds this knowledge, or delays it, can be said to love his neighbour as himself. He, that voluntarily continues ignorance, is guilty of all the crimes which ignorance produces; as to him, that should extinguish the tapers of a lighthouse, might justly be imputed the calamaties of shipwrecks. Christianity is the highest perfection of humanity; and as no man is good but as he wishes the good of others, no man can be good in the highest degree, who wishes not to others the largest measures of the greatest good. To omit for a year, or for a day, the most efficacious method of advancing Christianity, in compliance with any purposes that terminate on this side of the grave, is a crime of which I know not that the world has yet had an example, except in the practice of the planters of America, a race of mortals whom, I suppose, no other man wishes to resemble.[3]

For professing Christians to keep subjugated peoples—Highlanders or Negro slaves—in ignorance of Christian truth is for Johnson a crime which no reasons of policy can justify.
  ' Johnson is thinking here of primitive peoples *already* subjugated to Christian influence. But where the initial act of

subjugation involves European colonial or imperial ambition, Johnson is basically an anti-imperialist, a "little Englander." Since the days of Columbus, European expansion had been accompanied by so many acts of greed and cruelty that Johnson could not wish well to it even though it had brought Christianity to those who had never heard of it. Because Johnson believes no man can predict the future course of history,[3a] he is never tempted to argue that the ultimate conversion of all men to Christianity is a part of God's plan—it may or may not be. In the note to *Irene* referred to above, Johnson writes that "the Extent of this Religion [he probably means Islam] can be no argument, because though only one Religion can be true . . . no one takes in the greatest part of Mankind. Mysterious Providence suffers Man to be in Darkness" (*Poems*, pp. 358-59). Johnson has obviously considered the argument that the "extent" of any religion may be evidence of its truth; indeed, Johnson uses this argument himself when he infers the truth of Christianity from its early, rapid expansion.[3b] But the early Christian centuries were now at an end. Since then a new religion, Islam, had spread over great parts of the earth, and Johnson, dramatizing in *Irene* an episode of its expansion at the expense of Greek Christianity, was hardly the man to indulge himself in visions of a world ultimately Christian. And so he is never tempted to condone the evils of colonialism because of a supposed greater good, the expansion of Christianity.

But we may safely say that even had Johnson found in his Bible or elsewhere good reason for believing in the ultimate Christianization of the world, he would never have hedged on the ends-means problem. One may not exploit, rob, enslave—and then plead the "will of God" or the "conversion of the heathen." Johnson's position is well expressed in Imlac's advice to Nekayah:

> When we act according to our duty, we commit the event to him, by whose laws our actions are governed, and who will suffer none to be finally punished for obedience. When, in prospect of some good, whether natural or moral, we break the rules prescribed us, we

withdraw from the direction of superiour wisdom, and take all consequences upon ourselves. Man cannot so far know the connexion of causes and events, as that he may venture to do wrong, in order to do right.

Or again, praising Soame Jenyns' "account of the essence of vice and virtue," Johnson adds

that the consequences of human actions being sometimes uncertain, and sometimes remote, it is not possible, in many cases, for most men, nor in all cases, for any man, to determine what actions will ultimately produce happiness, and, therefore, it was proper that revelation should lay down a rule to be followed, invariably, in opposition to appearances, and, in every change of circumstances, by which we may be certain to promote the general felicity, and be set free from the dangerous temptation of *doing evil that good may come.*[4]

Johnson's italics refer to Romans 3:8 where St. Paul pronounces damnation on those who say, or suspect Christians of saying, "Let us do evil, that good may come." And the rule of revelation, the test of a man's actions is, as Jenyns says, "doing good, that is, cooperating with his creator, as far as his narrow sphere of action will permit, in the production of happiness. And thus the happiness and misery of a future state will be the just reward or punishment of promoting or preventing happiness in this."[5] Because Johnson believes Christians are forbidden by the New Testament to use un-Christian means, whatever the ends in view, he has considerable difficulty when faced with Christianity in its more militant role. His comment on the Crusades is a case in point:

The lawfulness and justice of the holy wars have been much disputed; but perhaps there is a principle on which the question may be easily determined. If it be part of the religion of the Mahometans to extirpate by the sword all other religions, it is, by the law of self-defense, lawful for men of every other religion, and for Christians among others, to make war upon Mahometans, simply as Mahom-

etans, as men obliged by their own principles to make
war upon Christians, and only lying in wait till opportunity shall promise them success.[6]

Johnson can justify the Crusades only by pretending that it
was a matter of self-preservation. That he was concerned to
defend the Crusades *at all* was due, I think, to his reluctance
to believe that events of such importance to Christian history
were difficult to justify on moral or religious grounds. Since
he can defend the aggressive militancy of the Crusaders only
by recourse to that ultimate appeal, the right of self-preservation, his comment, I would argue, is a kind of reflection in
reverse of his own belief, so eloquently expressed in the
preface to Lobo, that violence and aggression are contrary to
the whole spirit of Christianity.

In any case, Johnson's remark on the Crusades should not
be understood as an accurate reflection of his attitude toward
Islam. He once said "there are two objects of curiosity,—the
Christian world, and the Mahometan world. All the rest may
be considered as Barbarous" (IV, 199). That word "curiosity"
more accurately sums up Johnson's attitude toward Islam, and
Johnson's curiosity is largely free from bigotry or prejudice.
He wishes to understand Mohammedanism, not to score de-
bating points against it. At his death Johnson's library contained (item 69) George Sale's excellent English translation of
the Koran (1734), and Sale's long "Preliminary Discourse,"
the standard account of Mohammedanism in eighteenth-
century England, was by far the fairest, most impartial account
of Islam to appear in Johnson's century. (Gibbon, indeed,
called Sale "half a Mussulman.")[7] Johnson's work on *Irene*,
including his reading of Knolles's *Generall Historie of the
Turkes* and other books, gave him a better than average knowledge of "the Mahometan world." What seems clear is that
Johnson's attitude is not aggressive but defensive, as in this
remark to a friend departing for Aleppo—"Let the blindness
of Mahometans confirm you in Christianity" (Letter 598). The
Ottoman Empire was not yet the "sick man" of Europe, and
in the 1770's a Greek revolt against Turkish rule was bloodily

suppressed, a circumstance Johnson may have had in mind when he remarked that "there is no permanent national character; it varies according to circumstances. Alexander the Great swept India: now the Turks sweep Greece" (II, 194).

As "there is no permanent national character," so I find no indication that Johnson thought in terms of a permanent *religious* character. Whatever his opinion of the professed tenets of Islam, Johnson does not appear to believe that Mohammedans are more ferocious or bloody-minded than other people (at least Mahomet in *Irene*, tyrant though he is, has no thought of "extirpating" his newly acquired Christian subjects). In short, the Johnsonian belief that human nature is everywhere much the same holds true here also; that is, he finds nothing in Islam as a religion which produces a distinctive type of character or personality in its adherents. Certainly there is no distinctively Mohammedan character or personality type in *Irene* any more than a distinctively "Christian" type. The motives that move Greeks and Turks alike are those that animate all men regardless of religion. This drama, like so much of Johnson's work, reflects his conviction "that wherever human nature is to be found, there is a mixture of vice and virtue, a contest of passion and reason."[8] *Irene* is a comment on general human nature, not a study of rival religious ideologies.

Of course there are great differences between the Mohammedan and Christian worlds. There is the "arbitrary Pow'r" of Mahomet's government as contrasted with English liberty, but there is no indication that Johnson made any connection between Islam as a religion and the political or cultural tradition of oriental despotism. When Johnson seeks to explain English "liberty," he most often refers it to a thoroughly secular cause, to commerce and trade, which encourage it. In short, there is no indication that Johnson thought of Christianity, Islam, or any other religion as more favorable per se to one type of political system than another. Again, while Johnson considers "the natives of the Mahometan empires" to "approach most nearly to European civility," he finds they "have no higher pleasure at their convivial assemblies than to hear a piper, or gaze upon a tumbler," but these pleasures have nothing to do with the character of their religion, but with the fact that, lacking newspapers and other means of "intelligence," the Mohammedans, like all men in such a situation, necessarily have recourse to pleasures which are "merely sensual" (*Works*, II, 23).

There is then no Christian, no Mohammedan, no "Bramin"[9] "human nature"; one is reminded again of Johnson's admission that the moralities of all religions are pretty much the same. As to the issue of religious truth, Johnson adopts the same attitude we have seen him take in his discussion of the Christian evidences. Certainly, he believes these evidences stronger than those in favor of any other religion, but no man can *demonstrate* the truth of any religion, and the "greatest part" of all knowledge, even for the learned, is "implicit faith." Hence Johnson can exclaim, "as to religion, have we heard all that a disciple of Confucious, all that a Mahometan, can say for himself?" the point being that the convert from one Christian sect to another necessarily acts without all the facts. Without an exhaustive knowledge of *all* religions, he is in no position to demonstrate the superiority of his own, whether this be the sect in which he has been educated or the sect to which he converts. So far as *this* consideration is a factor, he might just as well have adhered to the religion of his parents (III, 299). Thus the problem of religious truth is ultimately insoluble. At least Johnson sees no way of solving it by any means presently available to the finite human intellect. For the present at least, as between Christianity and the other world religions, the issue of religious truth is a matter which "Misterious Providence," for its own purposes, has hid "in Darkness."

Johnson refuses to speculate about these purposes. Accepting the fact that Christianity is not, and may never be, the predominant religion of mankind, Johnson's attitude toward Islam and other world religions may be fairly characterized as a "live and let live" attitude: he stands for a policy of peaceful coexistence, insofar as this is possible given the restless ambition of rulers and the other moral frailties which afflict all men regardless of religion.

The *first* duty of Christians is not the conversion of Moslems, "Bramins," American Indians, or anyone else. The first duty of Christians is to work out their own salvation in the "narrow sphere of action" in which Providence has placed them. As Johnson believes the age of miracles has passed (although he thinks miracles still possible), so, I think, he believes the great age of Christian missionary activity has passed into history, its object, the secure establishment of the Christian religion, having been achieved. Islam is now the chief rival to Christianity, but by no means a serious threat. It is "an object of curiosity," not a menace.

We may be a bit more specific concerning the attitude Johnson thinks Christians should adopt toward those of other religions. It may be inferred that Johnson would expect Christians placed in contact with those of other faiths to maintain the credit and honor of their religion by a high standard of personal conduct. Moreover, for Johnson, those in possession of religious truth bear a great responsibility. Faults excusable in those whom God has left in ignorance may not be excused in those who know the truth. Thus, "bad men with the instructions of true Religion, are worse [than] Bad men with a worse Religion." Relevant in this connection is Irene's speculation that the Supreme Being may

> accept of Virtue whatever outward circumstances it may
> be accompanied with, and may be delighted with Varieties
> of Worship, but is Answer'd That Variety cannot affect
> that being who infinitely happy in his own perfections
> wants no external gratifications, nor can infinite . . . Truth
> be delighted with falsehood. that though he may guide
> or pity those he leaves in Darkness. he abandons those
> who shut their eyes against the beams of Day. (*Poems*,
> pp. 360, 363)

Apostasy is thus a very serious matter, but what Johnson recognizes in the case of change of sect among Christians he recognizes also in the more serious instance of apostasy from Christianity to "false" religion. Johnson believes it likely that in most instances the convert from one Christian sect to another is, at worst, converting from a "purer," more "rational" version of Christian truth to one less pure and less rational. This is bad enough, but the Christian who converts to Islam or to any other non-Christian religion exchanges truth for error, a much more serious offense.

Nevertheless, Johnson recognizes the possibility that as changes of sect among Christians may be honestly or dishonestly motivated, the same is true of conversions to non-Christian religions. And so he is careful to indicate that Irene's conversion is *not* honestly motivated, that, as Mustapha says, "Those pow'rful Tyrants of the Female Breast / Fear and Ambition, urge her Compliance," and Mustapha, the virtuous Mohammedan, expresses his own "scorn" for the "beautiful Apostate" since Irene will be receiving the "Prophet's Law" for the wrong reasons: "Heav'n will contemn the mercenary Fervours, / Which Love of Greatness, not of Truth, inflames." The point is that Johnson, consistently with his own principles, could hardly have condemned Irene if her apostasy had been based upon love of truth, that is, upon honest religious conviction. However deplorable, such an apostasy would have to be classified as an honest error, not as a crime, and because Johnson wants Irene's apostasy to appear *as* a crime, he is careful to make it apparent that "pious Warmth" for the "Prophet's Law" has nothing to do with her decision.

Thus the same motivations, the same mixture of virtue and vice, the same possibilities for good and evil which Johnson finds among Christians, he finds operative in the non-Christian world. The differences between these two worlds, admittedly great, are for Johnson cultural, not psychological, differences, or, as I have said, there is for Johnson no Christian, no Moslem, no "Bramin" "human nature."

Critics like Bate and Voitle, emphasizing the greatness of Johnson as moralist, as perceptive analyst of human behavior and motivation, proceed on the assumption that Johnson's success in this area is due to his powers of observation. If Johnson concludes that men are everywhere much the same, that they share a common human nature, this is a conclusion drawn from the consideration of many individual instances. Johnson reaches this conclusion empirically, inductively; his very success as a moralist owes much to the fact that the reader senses the weight of many particular "observations," as it were, behind Johnson's various generalizations concerning human behavior as a whole. Of course, Bate and Voitle realize that Johnson is a believer in moral absolutes, but neither critic is primarily concerned with the connection between this belief and Johnson's success as an "empirical" moralist, that is, as a man whose shrewd analyses of human behavior were "dictated by his own profound and hardheaded knowledge of the nature of man,"[10] a knowledge gained largely through experience and observation.

There can be no doubt that Johnson's knowledge was gained in precisely this way. Moreover, if Johnson convinces us that he knows human nature better than most men, this is due to Johnson's own powers of mind and perception; it is not due to his belief in moral absolutes or to any other aspect of his religious belief as such. Nevertheless, a twentieth-century scientist or secular humanist, aware of great variations in patterns of human conduct and behavior through the centuries, might well ask Voitle what he means when he talks about Johnson's knowledge of the "nature of man." What does "man" mean here? Eighteenth-century man, "civilized" man, European man, or all men, including fifteenth-century Moslems and twentieth-century Trobriand Islanders?

This is not a quibble; what I am concerned to point out is that Johnson is a moral absolutist, not a moral relativist, and that he could hardly be otherwise, given his Christian orthodoxy, whatever his purely experiential conclusions concerning "the nature of man." Johnson's Christian anthropology, derived from his understanding of Genesis, tells him there is a common human nature, that this includes a common *moral* nature, or, more specifically, that all men are endowed by God with the ability to distinguish good from evil.[10a] But this implies something really there to be distinguished; that is, the existence of an *objective* moral order in the world, or, as C. S. Lewis puts it, a "Law of Right and Wrong," a "Law of Decent Behavior."[11]

Now the moral relativist, as I conceive of him here, would

agree that no society could exist without general agreement concerning standards of conduct (whatever the source, or sources, of this agreement). But he would go on to argue that because different peoples have had quite different moralities, it is meaningless to speak of an objective moral order, or a "Law of Right and Wrong." There is in fact no such law; there is only, as Jim Casey says in Steinbeck's *Grapes of Wrath*, "just stuff people do,"[12] and as the things people do vary widely in all societies, past and present, there is little or no evidence in favor of the proposition that men have a common moral nature. The moral relativist argues instead that men have common *needs* (material, social, sexual, especially psychological) and that these needs, at different times and in different cultures, produce widely different patterns of conduct. Hence there is no universal moral standard, no general agreement among men that certain actions are moral, other actions immoral.

But Johnson, I would argue, is a moral absolutist in the sense that he thinks men are now, and always have been, in general agreement concerning the morality or immorality of certain acts. At the same time Johnson, like the moral relativist, recognizes wide variations in patterns of conduct. Thus he allows "that a man who only does what every one of the society to which he belongs would do, is not a dishonest man. In the republick of Sparta, it was agreed, that stealing was not dishonourable, if not discovered. I do not commend a society where there is an agreement that what would not otherwise be fair, shall be fair; but I maintain, that an individual of any society, who practises what is allowed, is not a dishonest man." I have deliberately chosen an example in which Johnson would seem to approach the position of the moral relativist, but I call attention to the language he uses. What does he mean when he says stealing "would not otherwise be fair"? I suggest he means the Spartans themselves *know* stealing would not otherwise be fair. The Spartans themselves are in the position of the man who lies and *knows* he lies; they recognize the existence of a moral law while agreeing to violate it. The fact that they do violate it is consistent with Johnson's belief in free will; had he cared to, he might have cited the Spartans as evidence in favor of Christianity. Thus, on another occasion, he remarks that "the happiness of society depends on virtue. In Sparta, theft was allowed by general consent: theft, therefore, was *there* not a crime, but then there was no security; and what a life they must have had, when there was no security."[13] Johnson might have argued that the Spartan instance is exceptional even in pagan antiquity, and thereby in itself evidence of a general belief among men that stealing is wrong, but such a flagrant and wholesale violation of the moral law is more easily accounted for in pagan than in Christian societies, since in the former most men are unaware of the divine condemnation of such acts. The moral law exists, and is known, but as it exists without its proper basis, the "fear and love of God" as Christians understand it, it is frequently violated.

If Johnson is a moral absolutist in the sense outlined here, this is only to say that he accepts an ancient and orthodox Christian view. Of course, a belief in the essential uniformity, including the *moral* uniformity, of human nature is a part of the eighteenth-century *Weltgeist* and is hardly to be accounted for in terms of religion. The idea of a general human nature underlying all cultural and historical differences is pervasive in Johnson's century: it is one reason why the more respectable of Gibbon's Roman emperors seem to have something in common with the enlightened despots of eighteenth-century Europe. But if Christians and philosophes alike share this view, it is at least worth pointing out in a book on Johnson's religion that this aspect of enlightenment thought—if such it be—is quite in harmony with traditional Christian teaching, whatever the satiric, anti-Christian purposes it may serve in the writings of a Voltaire or a Gibbon. This conception may be used to expose the parochial barbarity of Christian customs and "superstitions," as when the Chinese or Persian sage, in the typical enlightenment essay, laughs at the ridiculous Europeans, or it may be used to suggest that other peoples are not, after all, very different from those of Christian Europe, as in Johnson's remark that Lobo has "no Hottentots without religion" and "no Chinese perfectly polite."

I believe it impossible to determine in Johnson's case how far his own view represents an empirical conclusion, arrived at through his experience of life, how far it reflects the eighteenth-century *Weltgeist*, and how far it is an assumption derived from Johnson's belief that man is made in the image of God, and hence endowed with a certain moral nature. My own view is that all these factors operate simultaneously, that there is a constant, effortless (and unconscious) interaction among them. No one factor seems in conflict with the others. For Johnson, it would seem, experience, history, and religion teach the same lesson, "that certain general principles and concepts of the moral order are common to all peoples at all times."[14]

X

Conclusion:
A Religious View of Life

JOHNSON's *Adventurer* essay 107 concludes with the following
paragraph:

> Life is not the object of science: we see a little, very
> little; and what is beyond we can only conjecture. If we
> enquire of those who have gone before us, we receive
> small satisfaction; some have travelled life without obser-
> vation, and some willingly mislead us. The only thought,
> therefore, on which we can repose with comfort, is that
> which presents to us the care of Providence, whose eye
> takes in the whole course of things, and under whose
> direction all involuntary errors will terminate in happiness.

"Science" here means "knowledge," and Johnson has been
arguing that human wisdom can never point to one mode of
life as superior to another. What brings happiness to one man
is misery for his neighbor: one man "hastens to chuse a wife,
and the other laughs at his rashness or pities his ignorance;
yet it is possible that each is right, but that each is right only
for himself."

What I have tried to show in this book is that orthodoxy
is "right" for Johnson, that it is not at war with the innermost
needs or drives of his being. There is tension in Johnson's
faith, there are doubts and fears,[1] but at all major points

Johnson finds Christian doctrine and teaching so exactly consonant to the human condition that it is difficult to assume impulses in him constantly at war with his faith. Johnson's constant reiteration of his belief that religion is the only *rational* solution to the problem of human life—which is found *throughout* his writings—should not be understood as the expression of a pious hope, a kind of conventional apologetics intended to reconcile religion with reason. What Johnson is saying is that the more we learn of human nature, the more carefully we consider man in *all* his aspects, the more evident it becomes that the religious view of life is the only rational view, the only view that does not jar with the facts of experience, the only view, indeed, that really takes these facts into account. And the most important discovery we make, if we consider man as he really is and not as we might wish him to be, is that *all* his faculties—of mind, soul, or will—are such that "finite objects" can never satisfy them. This distinguishes man from "other creatures" and is for Johnson "a strong proof of the superior and celestial nature" of the human soul. As Johnson points out in *Rambler* 41, the beasts seem perfectly adapted to their environment. They seem

> always to be fully employed, or to be completely at ease without employment, to feel few intellectual miseries or pleasures, and to have no exuberance of understanding to lay out upon curiosity or caprice, but to have their minds exactly adapted to their bodies, with few other ideas than such as corporeal pain or pleasure impresses upon them.

Hence we have no reason to believe they have "higher faculties, or more extensive capacities, than the preservation of themselves or their species, requires."

How different is man! For Johnson it is simply a fact of experience that man is hardly ever satisfied with the present, that he is forced "to have recourse, every moment, to the past and future for supplemental satisfactions." Present happiness is momentary and fleeting; we must look to the past or to the future to "relieve the vacuities of our being, by recollection of former passages, or anticipation of events to come." Man, then, is *not* adapted to his environment. Very few of his "hours" are "filled up with objects adequate" to his mind.

Secularism flounders because it fails to take these facts into account. It attempts to "adjust" man to his finitude. But the attempt is vain because it involves a misconception concerning the true nature of mind, soul, and will. Religion, on the other hand, sees the true implications of man's finitude; it traces his misery to its true source, and its doctrine of a future life is a rational recognition of the fact that man in this life is dependent and incomplete. Nor can man by taking thought ever alter his limited nature. Growth in wisdom and self-control (stoicism) can never change the fact of man's dependence and incompleteness, for these are the qualities that make man human, that distinguish him from the beasts. The beasts are self-sufficient; man is not. But this weakness is also man's glory, a sign of his transcendent destiny. And so, in another sense, "life is not the object of science." But life *is* the "object" of religion, for religion exists to fulfill man, to complete him, to give him finally his true "nature," his true "life."

At the same time it is true that Johnson's famous scepticism extends far beyond a reluctance to credit extraordinary events. He is sceptical about a number of matters of considerable importance to orthodox Christianity. Johnson thinks created wisdom can give no satisfactory solution to the problems of evil and free will; he thinks no man can have the same conviction of the truth of religion that he has in the common affairs of life; nor does he believe that "philosophy" can ever give a satisfactory account of the Christian revelation as following, necessarily or contingently, from the nature of God or of the universe.

But I think it no paradox to affirm that these scepticisms, instead of weakening Johnson's religious faith, rather act to confirm it. In the first place, these negative conclusions are "hardly won." They reflect, not what Johnson wished to believe, but what he was forced to believe (although he was more easily reconciled to some of them than to others). But once thought through and accepted, these negative conclusions are seen to be in harmony with the hard facts of everyday experience. They lead Johnson to the conclusion, not that religion is "unreasonable," but that human reason is limited. If, as Johnson thought, reason is often ineffective in coping with the minor problems of day-to-day existence, it is hardly cause for wonder that he finds it helpless to give satisfactory answers to problems of far greater complexity. And if reason is limited at every turn, this fact of experience is confirmed by revelation, which insists that in this earthly life we "see through a glass, darkly," we know but "in part" (I Cor. 13:12). This is not fideism. We have already seen that Johnson believes unaided reason capable of limited discoveries concerning the "things of God." Johnson is simply facing up to the fact that in certain areas of speculation definitive conclusions can never be reached. But if the mind is limited, if it torments itself seeking solutions to problems it can never solve, this is only to be expected since, for Johnson, *all* our faculties too often serve but for our torment. *All* of life is involved in "perplexity." One of our most important secular concerns is our choice of a profession, provided we are in a position to choose. But "life is not the object of science." There are no principles by which we can determine a priori what profession brings the greater happiness, nor can we ever be sure that our own particular choice will bring the satisfactions we might reasonably expect from it.

This fact in itself would pose no insuperable difficulty if men were not constantly deluding themselves into the belief that finite objects can bring a happiness which belongs only to the life eternal. Men *do* have "intimations of immortality." They can imagine a kind of felicity which, in duration and intensity, partakes of that eternal joy which—their reason *should* tell them—can never be theirs under the limitations of finite existence. The rational man, the man of religious faith, makes this inveterate tendency of his nature work for him, not against him. His faith enables him to exercise some control over his dreams of earthly felicity; he is therefore less subject to the constant disappointment of expectation that must afflict the man who has no faith in a future state of "compensation." And so *Rasselas* is one long, persistently argued endeavor to show that finite objects can never finally satisfy, but *not* by reason of any defect in the object. The defect—and the glory —is in man himself, a finite creature ever yearning for infinite satisfactions. And so the only rational "choice of life" is the "choice of eternity," a "mode of existence which shall furnish employment for the whole soul, and where pleasure shall be adequate to our powers of fruition" (*Works,* II, 117).

This argument for the religious view of life is, in one sense, strikingly "modern." From the nature of man, from his weakness, from his finitude, from his alienation, from his "un-fitness" for this life, Johnson argues for the existence of the supernatural. The argument is from the nature of man to the existence of God, and this in essence is the argument of many theologians today who face a theology without proofs. These apologists assert with Johnson that man is not the tool-making animal, nor even the reasoning animal, that he is, instead, the religious animal. He may bow the knee to false gods, to the gods of pleasure, money, power, political party, nation, race— so Tillich—but a god he will have. It is a matter of choosing the right one: seek and ye shall find. And for Johnson the right choice involves the highest exercise of human reason:

> Moving through the mists of earthly hope and fear, man becomes capable of religious hope and fear—the ultimate tests of rationality. Johnsonian man is a son of Adam in that his primary impulse is toward selfishness and pride, toward faction, disagreement, excess, particularity, roman-tic escape, illusion, obsession, ultimate madness. But he is also potentially saved, for the faculty of reason in him, exercised through initial free choice, makes possible moral commitment, humility (in the widest religious sense), patience, realism, fulfillment of duty, "usefulness," salvation.[2]

The Johnsonian argument outlined in these concluding pages is "modern" because perennial, and perennial because it is really an argument about the nature of man. And because the nature of man is an inexhaustible subject, the question is still with us—the debate continues.

Notes

PREFACE

1. Compare Boswell: "there was hardly any topick, *if not one of the great truths of Religion and Morality*, that he might not have been incited to argue, either for or against it" (*Life*, III, 24, my italics).

2. See Voitle's review of Quinlan's book in *Journal of English and Germanic Philology*, LXIV (1965), 322-24.

CHAPTER I

1. Hawkins, *Life of Samuel Johnson* (London, 1787), p. 3; *Life*, I, 37.

2. Greene, p. 47.

3. *Thraliana*, ed. Katharine C. Balderston (Oxford, 1951), I, 159.

4. Clifford, p. 10.

5. Sir Charles Petrie, *The Jacobite Movement: The Last Phase* (London, 1950), p. 181.

6. *Works*, I, 10.

7. *Johnsonian Gleanings* (London, 1909-52), III, 62.

8. Clifford, p. 22.

9. Greene, p. 49.

10. All references to the *Whole Duty* are to the London edition of 1684 with citations to chapter and section.

11. John Nichols, *Literary Anecdotes of the Eighteenth Century* (London, 1812), II, 600.

12. L. E. Elliott-Binns, *The Early Evangelicals: A Religious and Social Study* (London, 1955), p. 402.

13. *Johnsonian Gleanings*, X, 27.

14. *Works*, I, 6, 134; Greene, p. 50.

15. W. E. H. Lecky, *England in the Eighteenth Century* (New York, 1892), III, 15.

16. G. M. Trevelyan, *Blenheim* (London, 1948), pp. 68-69.

17. *Boswell's Note Book 1776-1777*, ed. R. W. Chapman (London, 1925), p. 20.

18. See my "Johnson's Prayer for Kitty Chambers," *Modern Language Notes*, LXXVI (1961), 216-17.

19. Charles Wheatly, *A Rational Illustration of the Book of Common Prayer* (London, 1852), p. 374. First published in 1710.

20. *Memoirs, Anecdotes, Facts, and Opinions*, 2 vols. in one (London, 1824), II, 152, 154.

21. Clifford, p. 19; *JM*, I, 161.

22. *Boswell's Note Book*, pp. 19-20.

23. E. C. Mossner, *The Life of David Hume* (Austin, Texas, 1954), p. 34.

24. G. M. Trevelyan, *The Peace and the Protestant Succession* (London, 1946), p. 164.

25. In April of 1781 Johnson "read the first Sunday in the Duty of Man" in which he "had till then only looked by compulsion or by chance." The editors of the Yale edition of Johnson's *Diaries* remark that Johnson has forgotten that he quoted "extensively" from the *Whole Duty* in the *Dictionary* (*Works*, I, 307). But this seems incorrect. Looking through the first edition of the *Dictionary* for other purposes, I recall no quotations from the *Whole Duty*. A rough check of the letter "A" indicates no quotations from the *Whole Duty* but many from two other works attributed to Allestree, the *Decay of Piety* (1667) and the *Government of the Tongue* (1674—there are at least

32 quotations from the *Decay of Piety*). This means, I think, that Allestree's brand of piety was highly congenial to Johnson, and that he was deterred from "looking into" the *Whole Duty* in later life, not because he thought the book defective in any way, but simply because of its association in his mind with irksome boyhood tasks.

26. C. J. Stranks, *Anglican Devotion* (London, 1961), p. 144.

CHAPTER II

1. Gordon W. Allport, *The Individual and His Religion* (New York, 1964), p. 32.

2. "Dr. Johnson's Troubled Mind," in *Samuel Johnson: A Collection of Critical Essays*, ed. Donald J. Greene (Englewood Cliffs, N.J., 1965), pp. 22-29.

3. See, respectively, *Works*, I, 7; *JM*, I, 163; Clifford, p. 75.

4. *Boswell's Note Book*, pp. 19-20.

5. *JM*, I, 157-58; Clifford, pp. 74-75.

6. Letter 772; *Life*, I, 63, n.1.

7. Clifford, pp. 91-92.

8. *Poets*, I, 182.

9. David Hume, *Dialogues concerning Natural Religion*, ed. N. K. Smith (2d ed.; New York, 1948), p. 6.

10. *The Existence of God* (Ithaca, N. Y., 1965), p. xii.

11. *Dialogues*, ed. Smith, p. 7.

12. *Life*, I, 445-46, n.3; 57.

13. Reade, *Johnsonian Gleanings*, V, App. K, pp. 213-29.

14. Matthew Prior, "To Dr. Sherlock, on his Practical Discourse concerning Death"; *Spectator* 289.

15. Albert Rosenberg, *Sir Richard Blackmore* (Lincoln, Neb., 1953), pp. 98-108.

16. *Poets*, III, 393-94.

17. Walker, *The Decline of Hell* (Chicago, 1964), pp. 22-23. For Adams, see *Life*, IV, 299.

18. *The Decline of Hell*, p. 262.

19. Johnson has Matthew 25 in mind when, after "passionately and loudly" expressing his fear that he may be sent to hell and "punished everlastingly," he adds that "my Redeemer has said that he will set some on his right hand and some on his left" (*Life*, IV, 299-300).

20. *Life*, II, 104-5; III, 200.

21. *Poets*, II, 254.

22. *Works of the English Poets*, ed. Alexander Chalmers (London, 1810), X, 331, 337.

23. Stranks, *Anglican Devotion*, p. 162.

24. *Works*, II, 486, n.9 (*Adventurer* 131).

25. Nichols, *Literary Anecdotes*, IV, 202-3, 214.

26. G. R. Balleine, *A History of the Evangelical Party in the Church of England* (London, 1908), p. 4.

27. A. L. Reade, "Michael Johnson and Lord Derby's Library," *Times Literary Supplement*, July 27, 1940, p. 363; Clifford, p. 70.

28. Clifford, p. 63.

29. *The Individual and His Religion*, p. 31.

CHAPTER III

1. *Boswell's Note Book*, p. 20.

2. Stranks, *Anglican Devotion*, p. 193.

3. Clifford, p. 127.

4. Elliott-Binns, *Early Evangelicals*, p. 310.

5. *Anglican Devotion*, p. 281.

6. *Early Evangelicals*, p. 275.

6a. *Anglican Devotion*, p. 281.

7. G. R. Cragg, *The Church and the Age of Reason* (Penguin Books, 1960), p. 150; *Early Evangelicals*, p. 186.

8. *Early Evangelicals*, p. 159.

9. *Early Evangelicals*, p. 406; S. G. Brown, "Dr. Johnson and the Religious Problem," *English Studies*, XX (1938), 9.

10. Katharine C. Balderston, "Doctor Johnson and William Law," *PMLA*, LXXXV (1960), 393.

11. *Samuel Johnson: A Layman's Religion*, p. 164.

12. "Doctor Johnson and William Law," p. 384.

13. *Life*, IV, 215, n.5; Clifford, p. 338 n.1; *JM*, II, 322.

14. *Life*, I, 64; Clifford, p. 129; Letter 772.

15. Greene, p. 67.

16. Quotations from Johnson's preface to Lobo are to *Works* (1825) V, 255-59.

17. Samuel Johnson, *A Voyage to Abyssinia* (London [actually Birmingham], 1735), pp. 59, 63. The above paragraph is based upon Greene, pp. 66-72.

18. Greene, p. 67.

19. Joachim Le Grand, *Voyage Historique d'Abissinie du R. P. Jerome Lobo* (Amsterdam, 1728), I, 2.

20. Johnson, *Voyage*, p. 338.

21. Greene, p. 72.

22. Gold, "Johnson's Translation of Lobo," *PMLA*, LXXX (1965), 61.

23. William Law, *A Serious Call to a Devout and Holy Life* (London, 1955), p. 283.

24. *Serious Call*, pp. 277-78. In the *Dictionary* Johnson distinguishes between the "theological virtue of universal love" and other senses of charity.

25. Michael Geddes, *The Church-History of Abyssinia* (London, 1696), p. 32; and compare Johnson's translation of Le Grand's tenth dissertation "On the Errors of the Abyssins relating to the Incarnation."

26. "Johnson's Translation of Lobo," p. 61.

27. Donald M. Lockhart believes Johnson later made such a special study for the Ethiopian background of *Rasselas*. Ludolf mentions works on Abyssinia by Alvares, Urreta, and Telles which Lockhart thinks Johnson used as sources for a number of details in *Rasselas*. (Ludolf's *History* was in Johnson's library—item 587.) There is no reason why Johnson could not have consulted

these—and a number of other works on Abyssinia listed in Lockhart's bibliography—during the period 1728-34. See Lockhart, " 'The Fourth Son of the Mighty Emperor': The Ethiopian Background of Johnson's *Rasselas*," *PMLA*, LXXVIII (1963), 516-28.

28. Cf. Johnson's prayer as he began work on the second volume of his dictionary: "O God who hast hitherto supported me enable me to proceed in this labour & in the Whole task of my present state that when I shall render up at the last day an account of the talent committed to me I may receive pardon for the sake of Jesus Christ" (*Works*, I, 50). Cf. also *Rambler* 77: "*Of him to whom much is given, much shall be required* [Luke 12:48]. Those whom God has favoured with superior faculties, and made eminent for quickness of intuition, and accuracy of distinctions, will certainly be regarded as culpable in his eye, for defects and deviations which, in souls less enlightened, may be guiltless." In 1768 Johnson prayed, "O God, make me to remember that *the night cometh when no man can work*," the quotation—St. John 9:4—being the same as that inscribed on Johnson's watch, which was new this year (*Works*, I, 118).

CHAPTER IV

1. *JM*, I, 256.

2. Donald and Mary Hyde, "Dr. Johnson's Second Wife," in *New Light on Dr. Johnson*, ed. F. W. Hilles (New Haven, 1959), p. 146.

3. *Works*, I, 52.

4. *Letters of Samuel Johnson*, ed. G. B. Hill (New York, 1892), I, 48 n.2.

5. *JM*, I, 256.

6. *An Account of the Life of Dr. Samuel Johnson*, ed. Richard Wright (London, 1805), pp. 123-24. Miss Boothby's letters to Johnson are cited hereafter in the text by page references to this work.

7. *JM*, I, 57.

8. "A discourse on the benefit which the holy spirit of God is of to man, in his journey through life," in William Romaine, *Works* (London, 1821), IV, 275. Page references in the text are to Vol. IV of this edition.

Notes

8a. The "Advertisement" reads as follows: "I have Nothing to say by way of Preface or Introduction. I only ask this Favour of the Reader, that he would not pass any Censure upon this Book, from only dipping into this, or that particular Part of it, but give it one fair Perusal in the Order it is written, and then I shall have neither Right, nor Inclination to complain of any Judgment he shall think fit to pass upon it" (Law, *Works* [London, 1892], VI, 55).

9. See Stephen Hobhouse, *Selected Mystical Writings of William Law* (London, 1948), p. 324.

10. *Works*, VI, 99-100.

11. *Letters of Samuel Johnson* (ed. Hill), I, 48 n.4.

12. *JM*, I, 257.

13. I have argued elsewhere on the basis of the phrase "forgive and accept my late conversion" from Johnson's last prayer, and from Hawkins' account of a religious experience Johnson had in February 1784, that in the last months of his life Johnson adopted a view of conversion not unlike that held by many Evangelicals. Even if one grants what I think doubtful, that Johnson adhered to the *necessity* of the sudden or "felt" conversion after this date, I find no evidence that he did so at any time *prior* to his February experience. This change of outlook, then, would seem to apply only to the last ten months of Johnson's life. Important as the February experience is for an evaluation of Johnson's *final* religious outlook, it would be important for the purposes of this book only if one believed—as I cannot —that for most of his mature life Johnson pinned his hopes for salvation upon the belief that an experience similar to the one he actually underwent in 1784 was an essential part of any "acceptable" conversion. See my "Samuel Johnson's 'Wonderful' Experience," *Johnsonian Studies* (Cairo, 1962), pp. 51-60, and "Samuel Johnson's Religious Development," *Studies in English Literature*, IV (1964), 457-74. For views different from mine and from each other, see Donald J. Greene, "Dr. Johnson's 'Late Conversion': A Reconsideration," *Johnsonian Studies* (Cairo, 1962), pp. 61-92, and the final chapter of Quinlan's *Samuel Johnson: A Layman's Religion.*

Nothing I have said in this chapter, or elsewhere in this book, should be understood as a denial that Johnson believed in the reality of supernatural "inspiration." Like orthodox Christians everywhere, Johnson prayed for the inspiration of God's

Holy Spirit. But how does he conceive of it? Two definitions from the *Dictionary* are relevant here. One definition of "inspiration" is "infusion of ideas into the mind by a superiour power," and under this Johnson quotes Watts: "*Inspiration* is when an overpowering impression of any proposition is made upon the mind by God himself, that gives a convincing and indubitable evidence of the truth and divinity of it: so were the prophets and apostles *inspired*." Now this, I suggest, is Miss Boothby's "divine evidence for divine truths." The point is not whether Johnson accepts the possibility of such inspiration—obviously he does—but whether he thought such gifts of the Holy Spirit were ordinarily granted to Christians of his own day, however devout. How many "prophets and apostles" did he see about him? Better as an indication of the kind of inspiration Johnson expected to receive—and we may hope often *did* receive—is a quotation from the *Decay of Piety* under "inspirit": "It has pleased God to *inspirit* and actuate all his evangelical methods by a concurrence of supernatural strength, which makes it not only eligible but possible; easy and pleasant for us to do whatever he commands us."

The language here, it seems to me, implies something altogether "quieter" and less dramatic than the kind of experience Miss Boothby, Romaine, and Law have in mind. Perhaps Johnson would have ascribed the "radiations of comfort" he experienced in church on Easter Day, 1776, and the "tender images" which "struck" him at Communion to "a concurrence of supernatural strength" (*Works*, I, 258-60). "Radiation" in the *Dictionary* is "emission of rays"—a quotation from Boyle under "radiate" may be pertinent here:

> Though with wit and parts their possessors could never engage God to send forth his light and truth; yet now that revelation hath disclosed them, and that he hath been pleased to make them *radiate* in his word, men may recollect those scatter'd divine beams, and kindling with them the topicks proper to warm our affections, enflame holy zeal.

CHAPTER V

1. J. W. Krutch, *Samuel Johnson* (New York, 1944), pp. 250-51.

2. *The Existence of God*, p. xii.

3. S. G. Brown, "Dr. Johnson and the Religious Problem," p. 17.

Notes

4. *Private Papers of James Boswell from Malahide Castle*, ed. G. Scott and F. Pottle (New York, 1928-34), XIV, 245.

5. *Works* (1825), VI, 75.

6. John Hick, *Faith and Knowledge* (Ithaca, N. Y., 1957), p. xi.

7. *Poets*, II, 205.

8. *Analogy of Religion* (London, 1906), p. xxvii.

9. See *Life*, III, 380; *JM*, II, 194.

10. "Dr. Johnson and the Religious Problem," p. 11.

11. *Works* (1825), VI, 19 (Review of *Four Letters from Sir Isaac Newton to Dr. Bentley*).

12. *Life*, V, 272; II, 8-9.

13. *Analogy* (1906), p. xxviii.

14. A rough count under the letter "L" in Johnson's *Dictionary* indicates 21 citations from Bentley's *Confutation of Atheism*, 21 from Ray's *Wisdom of God*, 12 from Burnet's *Sacred Theory of the Earth*, 6 from Derham's *Physico-Theology*, and 4 from Blackmore's *Creation*.

15. Richard Wollheim in his *David Hume on Religion* (Meridian Books, 1964), p. 21.

16. *A Demonstration of the Being and Attributes of God* (8th ed.; London, 1732), p. 127.

17. *Demonstration*, p. 334.

18. J. S. Whale, *The Protestant Tradition* (Cambridge, 1960), pp. 16-17.

19. See *Essays in Philosophy*, ed. Houston Peterson (Pocket Library, 1959).

20. Brown, "Dr. Johnson and the Religious Problem," p. 15.

20a. Cf. R. R. Palmer on the situation in eighteenth-century France: "Against unbelievers who had no . . . faith [in Catholicism] the argument of historical fact was undoubtedly the strongest that could be used. . . . The dominant school of apologists therefore undertook to prove religion by facts alone, to demonstrate empirically that a supernatural world existed" (*Catholics and Unbelievers in Eighteenth Century France* [Princeton University Press, 1939], p. 77).

t>4. *Private Papers of James Boswell from Malahide Castle*, ed. G. Scott and F. Pottle (New York, 1928-34), XIV, 245.

5. *Works* (1825), VI, 75.

6. John Hick, *Faith and Knowledge* (Ithaca, N. Y., 1957), p. xi.

7. *Poets*, II, 205.

8. *Analogy of Religion* (London, 1906), p. xxvii.

9. See *Life*, III, 380; *JM*, II, 194.

10. "Dr. Johnson and the Religious Problem," p. 11.

11. *Works* (1825), VI, 19 (Review of *Four Letters from Sir Isaac Newton to Dr. Bentley*).

12. *Life*, V, 272; II, 8-9.

13. *Analogy* (1906), p. xxviii.

14. A rough count under the letter "L" in Johnson's *Dictionary* indicates 21 citations from Bentley's *Confutation of Atheism*, 21 from Ray's *Wisdom of God*, 12 from Burnet's *Sacred Theory of the Earth*, 6 from Derham's *Physico-Theology*, and 4 from Blackmore's *Creation*.

15. Richard Wollheim in his *David Hume on Religion* (Meridian Books, 1964), p. 21.

16. *A Demonstration of the Being and Attributes of God* (8th ed.; London, 1732), p. 127.

17. *Demonstration*, p. 334.

18. J. S. Whale, *The Protestant Tradition* (Cambridge, 1960), pp. 16-17.

19. See *Essays in Philosophy*, ed. Houston Peterson (Pocket Library, 1959).

20. Brown, "Dr. Johnson and the Religious Problem," p. 15.

20a. Cf. R. R. Palmer on the situation in eighteenth-century France: "Against unbelievers who had no . . . faith [in Catholicism] the argument of historical fact was undoubtedly the strongest that could be used. . . . The dominant school of apologists therefore undertook to prove religion by facts alone, to demonstrate empirically that a supernatural world existed" (*Catholics and Unbelievers in Eighteenth Century France* [Princeton University Press, 1939], p. 77).

169

21. For the evidence see my "Johnson, Rousseau, and Religion," *Texas Studies in Literature and Language*, II (1960), 95-102.

22. *Life*, I, 444-45; III, 188.

23. Hume's *Dialogues*, ed. Smith, p. 50 n.3; John V. Price, *The Ironic Hume* (Austin, Texas, 1965), p. 53.

24. Letter 51.1.

25. Adams, *Essay*, p. 19.

26. *David Hume on Religion*, ed. Wollheim, p. 26.

27. Adams, *Essay*, pp. 17, 19.

28. *Essay on Truth* (2d. ed.; Edinburgh, 1771), p. 141.

29. *A History of British Philosophy to 1900* (Cambridge, 1965), p. 203. Published in book form in 1920, Sorley's work first appeared as separate chapters in the *Cambridge History of English Literature*.

30. Hume's *Dialogues*, ed. Smith, p. 50.

31. Quoted in E. C. Mossner, *The Life of Hume* (Austin, Tex., 1954), p. 289.

32. Quoted in N. K. Smith, *A Commentary to Kant's 'Critique of Pure Reason'* (2d. ed.; New York, 1950), p. xxviii n.1.

33. *Essay on Truth*, pp. 118-19.

34. E. A. Burtt, *Types of Religious Philosophy* (New York, 1951), p. 218.

35. *Dialogues*, ed. Smith, p. 53; *David Hume on Religion*, ed. Wollheim, pp. 22-23.

36. *Essay on Truth*, pp. 121-24.

36a. Cf. Sermon 7: "A contempt of the monuments and wisdom of antiquity, may justly be reckoned one of the reigning follies of these days, to which pride and idleness have equally contributed. The study of antiquity is laborious; and to despise what we cannot, or will not understand, is a much more expeditious way to reputation. Part of the disesteem into which their writings are now fallen, may indeed be ascribed to that exorbitant degree of veneration, in which they were once held by blindness and superstition. But there is a mean betwixt idolatry and insult, between weak credulity and total disbelief. The ancients are not infallible, nor are their decisions to be received without examination; but they are at least the determinations of men equally desirous with ourselves of discovering truth, and who had, in some cases, better opportunities than we now have." The "ancients" here are the Church Fathers, more especially "those . . . who lived in the ages nearest to the apostles" (*Works* [1825], IX, 356-57). For Johnson's extensive knowledge of the Church Fathers, see *Works*, I, 409-13.

37. Johnson used a similar argument against Boswell's contention that "the thought of annihilation gave Hume no pain": "It was not so, Sir. He had a vanity in being thought easy. It is more probable that he should assume an appearance of ease, than that so very improbable a thing should be, as a man not afraid of going . . . into an unknown state" (*Life*, III, 153). Johnson is probably thinking of Hume's own balancing of probabilities in the essay on miracles.

38. *Faith and Knowledge*, pp. xvi-xvii.

39. *The Career of Philosophy From the Middle Ages to the Enlightenment* (New York, 1964), p. 634.

40. *The English Moralists* (New York, 1964), p. 263.

CHAPTER VI

1. Voitle, *Samuel Johnson the Moralist* (Cambridge, Mass., 1961), p. 62. See also Bate, *The Achievement of Samuel Johnson* (New York, 1955).

2. For the importance Johnson attached to this commandment, see *Rambler* 81.

3. *Works* (1825), IX, 337-38.

3a. If Johnson's memory did not play him false, he was reading Mandeville's *Fable of the Bees* in 1728, the year of his encounter with Law's *Serious Call*. Mandeville, he remarked in 1778, "did not puzzle me; he opened my views into real life very much." But, insisting that "the happiness of society depends on virtue," Johnson said that the "fallacy" of Mandeville's book is "that Mandeville defines neither vices nor benefits. He reckons among vices every thing that gives pleasure. He takes the narrowest system of morality, monastick morality, which holds pleasure itself to be a vice, such as eating salt with our fish, because it makes it taste better; and he reckons wealth as a publick benefit, which is by no means always true. Pleasure of itself is not vice" (*Life*, III, 291-93).

In view of Professor Quinlan's emphasis upon the great influence of Law's *Serious Call* on Johnson, it is interesting to note a shrewd comparison of Mandeville and Law in Mrs. Thrale's diary for the year 1780:

> I have often mentioned how extreams meet: Law & Mandeville are not only of the same Opinion, but even use each other's Expressions in speaking of Pride & Humility; each splits upon the same Rock too, for failing to define Luxury or Temperance, they both leave their Readers uninform'd whether any thing but Acorns & Water are allowable to people of strict Virtue, which Mandeville holds to be perpetual Self denial; and says how many Trades are exercised to Obtain for Man the *Luxury* of *Small beer*. Law who was more delicate, considered *Friendship* as too luscious a Treat for a Christian & commands us to contract no particular kindness for any one or more Persons, but to love all Mankind alike, & in the same Degree:—forgetting that our Blessed Saviour *wept* for his Friend, & *loved* Lazarus & his Sisters with very particular & tender Regard. (*Thraliana*, I, 421-22)

It is at least within the realm of possibility that this comment, jotted down in her diary two years after Johnson's comment on Mandeville, may actually reflect Mrs. Thrale's recollection of a conversation with Johnson on this subject since she, like Johnson, accuses Mandeville of failing to define his terms. Moreover, at the same dinner party in which he discussed Mandeville, Johnson gave his assent to the same opinion concerning the "virtue" of friendship which Mrs. Thrale expresses. Arguing at first that the Christian doctrine of "universal benevolence" is contrary to the ordinary concept of friendship as a virtue, since friendship means "preferring the interest of a friend, to the neglect, or, perhaps, against the interest of others," Johnson expressed his entire approval of the counter-argument supplied by Mrs. Knowles, "the ingenious Quaker lady": "But, Doctor, our Saviour had twelve Apostles, yet there was *one* whom he *loved*. John was called 'the disciple whom JESUS loved'" (*Life*, III, 289-90).

At any rate, the parallel Mrs. Thrale draws between Law and Mandeville seems obvious enough. Would Johnson have failed to see that his criticism of Mandeville's "monastick" concept of morality might apply also to certain of the more rigorous prescriptions of Law in the *Serious Call?* If Johnson did see this, he may have taken a more critical attitude toward Law's doctrine of Christian perfection than Quinlan would allow for.

4. Sermon 3, *Works* (1825), IX, 311.

5. *JM*, II, 307.

6. Sermon 10, *Works* (1825), IX, 378.

7. *Rambler* 52. On Lipsius, see also *Works* (1825), VI, 284 *(Life of Boerhaave)*.

8. *Rambler* 32, and compare *Rambler* 6.

9. *Rambler* 52, 150.

10. *Samuel Johnson*, p. 1.

11. *Rambler* 47.

12. *Adventurer* 120.

13. *Idler* 12.

14. *Works* (1825), IX, 311.

15. *JM*, I, 241.

16. *Samuel Johnson the Moralist*, p. 179.

17. *Adventurer* 120.

18. *The Tragic Sense of Life*, tr. J. E. C. Flitch (Dover Publications, 1954), chap. 3.

19. Boswell, *Journal of a Tour to the Hebrides*, ed. F. A. Pottle and C. H. Bennett (New York, 1936), p. 155.

20. *The Tragic Sense of Life*, p. 47.

21. *Samuel Johnson: A Layman's Religion*, p. 135.

22. *The Tragic Sense of Life*, p. 51. To confine myself to Johnson's century, I find nothing "feeble" in Hume's resignation to "final death," which I regard as quite sincere, and Mossner's biography leaves no reason to believe that Hume was at all lacking in "life, health, and vitality."

23. *Samuel Johnson: A Layman's Religion*, p. 134.

24. See *Works* (1825), VI, 62 (Review of *A Free Enquiry into the Nature and Origin of Evil*).

25. *The Tragic Sense of Life*, p. 5.

CHAPTER VII

1. Hume, *Dialogues*, ed. Smith, p. 198.

2. *Works* (1825), VI, 47-76. Page references are inserted in the text.

3. Robert South, *Sermons Preached Upon Several Occasions* (Philadelphia, 1845), I, 241. Page references to this sermon (pp. 240-55) are inserted in the text.

4. *Works* (1825), IX, 314.

5. For instance, in *Free Will*, ed. S. Morgenbesser and J. Walsh (Englewood Cliffs, N. J.: Prentice-Hall, 1962).

6. Samuel I. Mintz, *The Hunting of Leviathan* (Cambridge, 1962), pp. 117-18.

7. *Demonstration*, 8th ed., p. 102: "*Man* also is by *necessity*, (not in the *nature of Things*, but though *God's appointment*) a *Free Agent.*"

8. *Demonstration*, pp. 104-5.

9. Eliot, "John Bramhall" in *Selected Essays* (3rd ed.; London, 1951).

10. F. A. Pottle, *James Boswell: The Early Years 1740-1769* (New York, 1966), pp. 32-33, 133.

11. Mintz, *Hunting of Leviathan*, p. 110.

12. Basil Willey, *The Eighteenth Century Background* (London, 1946), p. 4.

CHAPTER VIII

1. Greene, p. 236.

2. *Poets*, III, 53.

3. G. R. Cragg, *Puritanism in the Period of the Great Persecution* (Cambridge, 1957), p. 248.

4. *The Church and the Age of Reason* (Penguin Books, 1960), pp. 133, 135.

5. *Poets*, III, 13, n.1.

6. *The English Revolution 1688-1689* (New York, 1965), p. 86.

7. A. W. Evans, *Warburton and the Warburtonians* (London, 1932), p. 32.

8. *Reason and Authority in the Eighteenth Century* (Cambridge, 1964), pp. 199-200.

9. Evans, *Warburton*, pp. 32, 47.

10. For Johnson's opinion of the *Divine Legation*, see *Life*, IV, 48-49. The argument of the *Alliance* treatise is repeated in *Divine Legation*, Bk. 2, sects. 5-6. See Warburton's *Works* (London, 1811), II, 264-334.

11. *Warburton*, p. 33.

12. *Alliance* (*Works*, VII, 68).

13. *Alliance* (*Works*, VII, 56).

14. *Divine Legation*, Bk. 2, sect. 5 (*Works*, II, 288-89).

15. *Divine Legation*, Bk. 2, sect. 5 (*Works*, II, 287-88).

16. *Divine Legation*, Bk. 2, sect. 5 (*Works*, II, 292).

17. *Works* (1825), IX, 296, 500 (Sermons 1, 23, respectively).

18. *Poets*, I, 155-56.

19. Lecky, *History of England in the Eighteenth Century* (New York, 1893), VI, 26-27.

20. *Poets*, I, 214; *Works* (1825), IX, 61.

21. During the same year (1773) in which he expressed his satisfaction that the dissenters had gained no "immunities," he remarked, "You are frightened by what is no longer dangerous, like Presbyterians by Popery" (*Life*, V, 57).

22. It has been estimated that "by 1770 only one-half of the Presbyterian congregations remained orthodox on the Trinity." See Roland N. Stromberg, *Religious Liberalism in Eighteenth-Century England* (Oxford, 1954), p. 47 n.3.

23. *Poets*, I, 214-15.

23a. This, says Boswell, was his "usual remark" (*Life*, IV, 12).

23b. In the following passage Johnson praises the orthodox dissent of Watts and Mrs. Elizabeth Rowe (1674-1737): "They would have both done honour to a better society, for they had that charity which might well make their failings forgotten, and with which the whole christian world might wish for communion. They were pure from all the heresies of an age, to which every opinion is become a favourite, that the universal church has, hitherto, detested" (*Works* [1825], VI, 79). But Elwall, he said (*Life*, II, 251), "should have been put in the stocks." And Johnson's well known remark on Akenside's zeal for "liberty" reveals the close association he made between the ethos of dissent and social anarchy: "Whether, when Akenside resolved not to be a dissenting minister, he ceased to be a Dissenter, I know not. He certainly retained an unnecessary and outrageous zeal for what he called and thought liberty—a zeal which sometimes disguises from the world, and not rarely from the mind which it possesses, an envious desire of plundering wealth or degrading greatness; and of which the immediate tendency is innovation and anarchy, an impetuous eagerness to subvert and confound, with very little care what shall be established" (*Poets*, III, 411-12).

24. *Poets*, I, 108.

25. *Works* (1825), IX, 380.

25a. Cf. Johnson's attack on the Stage Licensing Act of 1737 in his *Compleat Vindication of the Licensers of the Stage* (1739).

26. *Samuel Johnson in Grub Street* (Providence, R. I., 1957), p. 247.

27. For Johnson, "rebellions and civil wars are the greatest evils that can happen to a people" (E. L. McAdam, Jr., *Dr. Johnson and the English Law* [Syracuse University Press, 1951] p. 97).

28. *Works* (1825), VI, 177 (*The False Alarm*).

29. *Poets*, II, 257; *Life*, II, 321.

30. Letter 785.

31. *Poets*, II, 257-58; Letter 803.

32. "But what must a philosopher think of those vain reasoners, who, instead of regarding the present scene of things as the sole object of their contemplation, so far reverse the whole course of nature, as to render this life merely a passage to something farther; a porch, which leads to a greater, and vastly different building. . . ." (*Enquiry concerning Human Understanding*, Sect. XI.)

CHAPTER IX

1. *Thraliana*, II, 707.

2. J. M. Osborn, "Dr. Johnson and The Contrary Converts," *New Light on Dr. Johnson* (New Haven, 1959), pp. 297-317.

3. *Life,* II, 27; Letter 184.

3a. Cf. Letter 308: "I think an unlimited promise of acting by the opinion of another so wrong that nothing, or hardly any thing can make it right. All unnecessary vows are folly, *because they suppose a prescience of the future which has not been given us"* (my italics).

3b. See above, p. 81.

4. *Works* (1825), I, 272; VI, 71.

5. *Works* (1825), VI, 71.

6. E. L. McAdam, Jr., *Dr. Johnson and the English Law* (Syracuse University Press, 1951), p. 186.

7. *Decline and Fall of the Roman Empire,* ed. William Smith (New York, n.d.) V, 205 n.65.

8. *Works* (1825), V, 256 *(Preface to Lobo).*

9. For Johnson on the "Bramins," see *Life,* IV, 12, 88.

10. Robert Voitle, *Samuel Johnson the Moralist* (Cambridge, Mass., 1961), p. 182. See also W. J. Bate, *The Achievement of Samuel Johnson* (New York, 1955).

10a. Cf. *Rambler* 6 (*Works* [1825], II, 25): "though the boast of absolute independence is ridiculous and vain, yet a mean flexibility to every impulse, and a patient submission to the tyranny of casual troubles, is below the dignity of that mind, which, however depraved or weakened, boasts its derivation from a celestial original, and hopes for an union with infinite goodness and unvariable felicity."

11. The terms are used *passim* in *Mere Christianity* (New York, 1958).

12. *The Grapes of Wrath* (New York, 1939), p. 32.

13. *Life,* II, 176; III, 293.

14. Art. "Ethics," *Catholic Encyclopedia* (New York, 1913), V, 557.

CHAPTER X

1. It may be appropriate to point out that "tension, doubts, and fears" are not, historically, a sign that one's Christian faith is weak or that one is temperamentally inclined to scepticism. Johnson had never heard of the modern theory that religion is

therapy, that its prime function is to induce "peace of mind" in the believer. To be sure, such peace of mind may be an important by-product of religious faith, and there is every indication that Johnson himself achieved some measure of it in the months prior to his death (see my "Samuel Johnson's 'Wonderful' Experience," *Johnsonian Studies* [Cairo, 1962], pp. 51-60). But I would agree with B. H. Bronson that, on the whole, religion for Johnson "was not a mild and sunny element in his life, but crossed with storm and struggle" (*Johnson Agonistes and Other Essays* [Berkeley, Cal., 1965], p. 41). But this has been true of many Christians, perhaps truer of those in the so-called Augustinian or Protestant tradition than of those in the Thomistic or Catholic tradition—as it may actually have been truer of Augustine and Luther than of Thomas Aquinas or Francis of Assisi. But one should be very cautious of generalization here—after all, it was not a Protestant who wrote *The Dark Night of the Soul*. The point is that doubts, even those which call in question the fundamentals of religious belief, are not in *themselves* reason for inferring a temperament "naturally" disposed to scepticism or free thought. As Christians, like other men, are of different temperaments, so it is only to be expected that for some of them religion should be a mild and sunny element in their lives, for others an element of storm and struggle.

2. Arieh Sachs, *Passionate Intelligence: Imagination and Reason in the Work of Samuel Johnson* (Baltimore, 1967), p. 110. The final chapter of Professor Sachs' book, from which I quote, entitled "The Rationality of Faith," seems to me an excellent statement, from another point of view, of the analysis I have presented in these concluding pages.

Index

Index